ISBN 978-1-330-11207-6
PIBN 10028608

Forgotten Books is a registered trademark of FB &c Ltd.
Copyright © 2017 FB &c Ltd.
FB &c Ltd, Dalton House, 60 Windsor Avenue, London, SW19 2RR.
Company number 08720141. Registered in England and Wales.

For support please visit www.forgottenbooks.com

English
Français
Deutsche
Italiano
Español
Português

www.forgottenbooks.com

Mythology Photography **Fiction**
Fishing Christianity **Art** Cooking
Essays Buddhism Freemasonry
Medicine **Biology** Music **Ancient
Egypt** Evolution Carpentry Physics
Dance Geology **Mathematics** Fitness
Shakespeare **Folklore** Yoga Marketing
Confidence Immortality Biographies
Poetry **Psychology** Witchcraft
Electronics Chemistry History **Law**
Accounting **Philosophy** Anthropology
Alchemy Drama Quantum Mechanics
Atheism Sexual Health **Ancient History**
Entrepreneurship Languages Sport
Paleontology Needlework Islam
Metaphysics Investment Archaeology
Parenting Statistics Criminology
Motivational

mer's day, were glad enough to resign to us.' Here is the same subtle law in operation. [Man often loves without knowing that he loves; and, little as he suspects it, he is deeply in love with his load.] He groans beneath it, as a man grumbles at the wife of his bosom, but, if it were taken from him, he would be almost as disconsolate as if *she* were taken from him.

When we were boys at school we learned ludicrous lessons about the weight of the air. How we laughed as we listened to the doctrines of Torricelli, and heard that every square inch of surface has to sustain a weight of fifteen pounds! How we roared in our rollicking scepticism when our school masters assured us that we were each of us being subjected to a fearful atmospheric pressure of no less than fourteen tons! But Mr. H. G. Wells has drawn for us a picture of men unladen. His heroes—Mr. Cavor and Mr. Bedford—have found their way to the moon. The fourteen tons of air are no longer on their shoulders. The atmospheric pressure is removed; they have lost their load, and they nearly lose their lives in consequence. They cannot control themselves. They can scarcely keep their feet on the soil. The slightest spring of the foot, and they bound like a ball into mid-air. If they attempt to leap over an obstructing boulder, they soar into space like larks, and land on a distant cliff or alight on an extinct volcano. Life becomes weird, ungovernable, terrible. They are lost without their load. Which things are symbolic. It is part of the pathos of mortality that we only discover how dearly we love things after we have lost them. We behold with surprise our affections, like torn and bleeding tendrils, hanging desolate, lamenting mutely the commonplace object about which they had entwined themselves. So is it with the lading and luggage of life. We never wake up to the delicious luxury of being heavily burdened until our shoulders miss the load that galled them. If we grasped the deepest philosophy of life a little more clearly we might perhaps fall in love with our luggage. The baby instinct is perfectly true. Our load is as essential to us as our lunch. Very few people have been actually crushed in this old world of many burdens. And those who have were not the most miserable of men. It will not be at all astonishing if the naturalists of to-morrow assure us that the animal world knows no transport comparable to the fierce and delirious ecstasy of the worm beneath the heel. It would only be a natural, and perfectly logical, advance upon our knowledge of Livingstone's sensations beneath the paw of the lion. At any rate, it is clear that man owes as much to his luggage as a ship owes to her keel. It seems absurd to build her delicately, and then burden her dreadfully. But the sailor loves the heavy keel and the full freight. It is the light keel and the empty hold that have most reason to dread the storm. Blessed be ballast! is a beatitude of the forecastle.

Such is the law of life's luggage. But the New Testament gives us a still loftier and lovelier word: 'Bear ye one another's burdens, and so fulfil the law of Christ.' And these laws—the law of nature and the law of Christ—are not conflicting, but concordant. The one is the bud, the other is the blossom. For Christ came, not to remove life's luggage, but to multiply our burdens. It is true, of course, that He said: 'Come unto Me, all ye that labour and are heavy laden,' but He only invited them that He might offer them His yoke and His burden. Here is something worth thinking about. Christ gives rest to the heart by giving burdens to the shoulders. And, as a matter of fact, it is in being burdened that we usually find rest. The Old Testament records the sage words of an old woman in addressing two younger ones: 'The Lord grant,' said Naomi, 'that ye may find rest, each of you, in the house of her husband!' Who ever heard of a woman finding rest *in the house of her husband?* And yet, and yet—! The restless hearts are not the hearts of wives and of mothers, as many a lonely woman knows. There is no more crushing load than the load of a loveless life. It is a burden that is often beautifully and graciously borne, but its weight is a very real one. The mother may have a bent form, a furrowed brow, and worn, thin hands; but her heart found its rest for all that. Naomi was an old woman; she knew the world very well, and her words are worth weighing. Heavy luggage is Christ's strange cure for weary hearts.

The law of life's luggage—the 'law of Christ'— has a racial application. It is notorious that a Christian people is not physically more robust than a savage people. Readers of Alfred Russel Wallace's *Travels on the Amazon* will remember that, the farther the intrepid voyager proceeded up the great waterway, the finer became the physique of the natives. And at last, when Dr. Wallace reached a point to which no white man had ever before penetrated, he discovered men and women any of whom might have posed as models for Grecian sculptors. The reason is obvious. The savage knows nothing of 'the law of Christ.' He will bear no other's burden. The sick must die; the wounded must perish; the feeble must go to the wall. Only the mightiest and most muscular survive and produce another generation. 'The law of Christ' ends all that. The luggage of life must be distributed. The sick must be nursed; the wounded must be tended; the frail must be cherished. These, too, must be permitted to play their part in the shaping of human destiny. They also may love and wed, and become fathers and mothers. The weaknesses of each are taken back into the blood of the race. The frailty of each becomes part of the common heritage. And, in the last result, if our men are not all Apollos, and if our women do not all resemble Venus de Medici, it is largely because we have millions with us who, but for 'the law of Christ,' operating on rational ideals, would have had no existence at all. In a Christian land, under Christian laws, we bear each other's burdens, we carry each other's luggage. It is the law of Christ, the law of the cross, a sacrificial law. The difference between savagery and civilization is simply this, that we have learned, in our very flesh and blood, to bear each other's burdens and so fulfil the law of Christ.

We set out with Dr. Guthrie. Let us return to him. He is excellent company. He is describing, with a glow of satisfaction, one of the ragged-schools he established in Edinburgh. 'I remember,' he says, 'going down the High Street early one morning and seeing a number of our children coming up. One of them was borne on the shoulders of another, and, on my asking the reason, he said that the little fellow had burned his foot the night before, and he was carrying him to school. That,' said the doctor emphatically, 'would not have happened in any other school in Edinburgh.' It is a parable. It is the law of life's luggage. It is the law of Christ. Christ carries our luggage so we can carry anothers.

~ Galatians 6:2

II

OUR DESERT ISLANDS

In childhood's golden hours we all of us squandered
a vast amount of sympathy upon Robinson Crusoe.
And in later years we have caught ourselves shed-
ding a silent tear for the sorrows of poor Enoch
Arden, imprisoned on his 'beauteous, hateful isle.'
In imagination, too, we have paced with the beloved
disciple the rugged hills of Patmos. We have even
felt a sympathetic pang for Napoleon in his cheer-
less exile at St. Helena. And all the while we have
clean forgotten that we ourselves are each of us
cast upon lonely, sea-girt islands. We are each one
of us hopelessly cut off, isolated and insulated.
Moreover, unlike the heroes of Defoe and Tenny-
son, we shall never sight a sail. Our beacon-fires
will never bring down any passing vessel to our
relief. It is for ever. At our very birth we were
chained, naked, like Andromeda, to our rock in mid-
ocean; and no Perseus will ever appear to pity and
deliver us. The links of the chain by which we are

Isrealites in the desert.

bound are many and mighty. At one or two of them it may do us good to look more particularly.

And by far the mightiest of these insulating factors is the mystery of our own individuality. *Western worldview vs. non western worldview* Each several ego is dreadfully alone in the universe. Each separate 'I' is without counterpart in all eternity. In the deepest sense we are each fatherless and childless; we have no kith or kin. When God makes a man He breaks the mould. Heaven builds no sister-ships. We may establish relationships of friendship and brotherhood with other island dwellers across the intervening seas. We may hear their voices shouted across the foam, and read and return their signals; but that is all. The most intense sympathy can never bridge the gulf. No man can enter into the soul of his brother man. 'I was in the isle,' says John. And he says it for us all. 'In all the chief matters of life,' says Amiel in his Journal, 'we are alone: we dream alone; we suffer alone; we die alone.' 'We are all islands,' says George Eliot in one of her beautiful letters to Mrs. Bray; 'each in his hidden sphere of joy or woe, our hermit spirits dwell and roam apart.' *loneliness is poverty* 'There is nothing more solemn,' says Dr. Alexander McLaren, 'than that awful loneliness in which each soul of man lives. We stretch out our hands and grasp live hands; yet there is a universe between the two that are nearest and most truly one.' And perhaps Matthew Arnold has said the last word when he sings:

> Yes, in the sea of life enisled,
> With echoing straits between us thrown,
> Dotting the shoreless, watery wild,
> We mortal millions live alone.

We have shed our tears over the terrific solitude of Robinson Crusoe and of Enoch Arden; and, in return, Robinson Crusoe and Enoch Arden urge us to weep for ourselves. For their partial and temporary solitude was as nothing compared with the absoluteness and permanence of our own.

But there are other insulating elements in life. Our very circumstances, being peculiar to ourselves, tend, of course, to cut us off from others. Our consciences, too, for there is nothing in the solar system so isolating as a secret, and especially as a guilty secret. A man with a secret feels that it cuts him sheer off from his fellows. A man with a guilty secret feels lonely in the densest crowd. A murderer can never find a mate. Civilization, therefore, tends to isolate us. Savages have but few secrets; they know each other too well. But we make secrets of everything. Our wealth, our poverty, our joys, our sorrows, are our own private affairs. The simplest question becomes an impertinence. To ask your next-door neighbour the dimensions of his bank balance, the sum of his weekly earnings, or the age of his wife, would stagger him more than a blow with a walking-stick. The conventionalities of civilized etiquette all separate us from each other, and we move in stately and solitary dignity through life to the watchword of 'Mind your own business!'

But by far the most tragic contributor to our isolation is our pitiful and pitiless lack of sympathy with each other. We may not altogether understand each other; and we have our revenge by taking some pains to misunderstand. Let me cull a pair of illustrations from familiar pages of our literature. (1) Robert Louis Stevenson tells a famous story of two maiden sisters in the Edinburgh of long ago. 'This pair,' he tells us, 'inhabited a single room. From the facts, it must have been double-bedded; and it may have been of some dimensions; but, when all is said, it was a single room. Here our two spinsters fell out—on some point of controversial divinity belike; but fell out so bitterly that there was never a word spoken between them, black or white, from that day forward. You would have thought that they would separate; but no, whether from lack of means, or the Scottish fear of scandal, they continued to keep house together where they were. A chalk line drawn upon the floor separated

How often many homes operate this way ...

their two domains; it bisected the doorway and the fireplace, so that each could go out and in, and do her cooking, without violating the territory of the other. So, for years, they co-existed in a hateful silence; their meals, their ablutions, their friendly visitors, exposed to an unfriendly scrutiny; and at night, in the dark watches, each could hear the breathing of her enemy. Never did four walls look down upon an uglier spectacle than these sisters rivalling in unsisterliness.' Here are desert islands for you! (2) In the *Romance of Religion*, Olive and Herbert Vivian tell a strange story of two nuns. They were Bernardines, and lived side by side for five years in two adjoining cells, and so thin a partition divided them that they could even hear the sound of each other's breathing. All this time they ate at the same table and prayed in the same chapel. At last one of them died, and, according to the rule of the Order, the dead nun was laid in the chapel, her face uncovered, and the Bernardines filed past, throwing holy water upon the remains as they went. When it came to the turn of the next-door neighbour, no sooner did she catch a sight of the dead nun's face than she gave a piercing shriek and fell back in a swoon. She had just recognized her dearest friend in the world, from whom she had parted in anger years before. Each had misunderstood the other, and thought the other unaffected by the quarrel. And for five years the two friends had lived side by side, neither having seen the other's face or heard the other's voice. So true are the tragic words of poor Tom Bracken—words that have an added pathos for those of us who knew something of the poet himself:

Not understood. We move along asunder;
　Our paths grow wider as the seasons creep
Along the years; we marvel and we wonder
　Why life is life, and then we fall asleep—
　　Not understood.

Not understood. How many breasts are aching
　For lack of sympathy. Ah, day by day,
How many cheerless, lonely hearts are breaking.
　How many noble spirits pass away—
　　Not understood.

O God! that men would see a little clearer,
　Or judge less harshly when they cannot see!
O God! that men would draw a little nearer
　To one another!—they'd be nearer Thee,
　　And understood.

'We are like islands,' says Rudyard Kipling, 'and we shout to each other across seas of misunderstanding.'

But there is another side to all, and happily a brighter one. Island life has its compensations. 'I was in the isle,' says John. But in the very next sentence he adds, 'I was in the Spirit.' Insulations

have their inspirations.   The world is not ruled by
its continents.   Wide continental areas, like China
and Russia, count for little in the world's history.
The continents are ruled by the islands, not the
islands by the continents.   'The ancient Grecians
and Phoenicians,' says Lamartine, 'imbibed some-
thing of the perpetual agitation and insubordination
of the sea.   The spectacle of the ocean renders man
more free and impatient of restraint, for he con-
stantly beholds the image of liberty in its waves, and
his soul imbibes the independence of the element.'
With which agrees a great American writer.   'It is
this fluid element,' he says, 'that gives fluidity
and progress to the institutions and opinions of the
race.   It is only in the great inland regions of the
world—in Central Africa and Asia—that bigotry
and inveterate custom have their seat.   In these vast
regions that never saw the sea men have lived from
age to age without progress or the idea of progress,
crushed under despotism and superstition, rooted
down like their trees, motionless as their mountains.
It was never a Babylon or a Timbuctoo or any city
of the inland regions that was forward to change or
improvement.   It was a Tyre, Queen of the Sea; a
Carthage, sending out her ships beyond the Pillars
of Hercules to Britain and the Northern Isles; an
Athens, an Alexandria,—these were the seats of

thought, of art, of learning, and literal improvement of every sort.' Island life has therefore compensations peculiar to itself. *Seasons of loneliness are in Preparation...*

All of which is an allegory. Every isolation is a preparation for the conquest of a continent. Think of the isolation of John Milton, represented by his blindness; and think, at the same time, of *Paradise Lost.* What an island Bedford Jail seemed to Bunyan! And what continents has he won by his *Pilgrim's Progress!* John fretted like a caged lion on his rock at Patmos; but his visions there have enriched every time and every clime. We are isolated in the loneliness of our own individuality that each individual may contribute out of his peculiar experience to the wealth of the whole world. There is no charge committed to our care so mysterious and so sacred as the development and diffusion of our own selves. And every other insulating element is designed, not as an exile for the one, but as an enrichment for the whole. The islands are the masters of the continents in this world and in every other. And thus it has come to pass that the dreariest, most desolate, and most awful isolation of which men have ever heard—the loneliness and dereliction of the Cross—is issuing, and must issue, in the conquest and redemption of the world.

OUR HIGHWAY ROBBERIES

Poor Mr. Little-Faith was violently assaulted and robbed in Deadman's Lane. So Bunyan tells us. But the remarkable thing about the crime was this, that, when he recovered his senses and was able to investigate his loss, he found that his assailants had taken only *his spending-money.* 'The place where *his jewels* were, they never ransacked; so those he kept still.' There is a subtle philosophy about the episode in Deadman's Lane. Prebendary Carlile, the head of the Church Army, tells a delightful story of a Welsh miner who, in the great days of the Revival, avowed himself a disciple of Jesus Christ. He had previously exhibited an amazing facility in the use of expletives of the baser kind. With his changed life, however, it became customary for him to meet the most exasperating treatment with a manly smile and a homespun benediction. His mates, disapproving the revolution in his behaviour, one day stole his dinner. But all they heard their transformed comrade say was: 'Praise the Lord!

18

[marginal note, left]: ...where your treasure is, there your heart will be also

[marginal note, right]: vehicle for living but not life itself?

I've still got *my appetite*! They can't take that!'
The good collier only emphasized, in his own quaint
way, the lofty logic of Deadman's Lane. The truth
is embedded in the very essence of Christian teach-
ing. The robbers always leave the best behind
them; they cannot help it. The writer of the Epistle
to the Hebrews commends his readers for having
taken joyfully the spoiling of their goods. And he
adds: 'Ye are well aware that ye have in your own
selves a more valuable possession, and one which
will remain.' Life's spoilers leave the best of the
spoil after all.

The pilgrims to the Celestial City must all of them
pass through the eerie shades of Deadman's Lane.
And they alone can enter that darksome avenue
with a song on their lips who are first assured of the
absolute security of their best possessions. In one
of the noblest passages of *Sesame and Lilies,* Ruskin
deals with that great saying in the Sermon on the
Mount concerning the treasures of the Court, which
a moth can destroy; the treasures of the Camp,
which rust can defile; and the treasures of the
Counting-house, which a thief can despoil. These,
then, are the desperadoes of Deadman's Lane—the
moth and the rust and the thief! And these are the
only things that they can steal—the treasures of
Place and of Power and of Pelf! But there must, as

Ruskin argues, be a fourth order of treasure—a web made fair in the weaving, by Athena's shuttle (a web that no moth can destroy); an armour forged in divine fire by Vulcanian force (an armour that no rust can defile); a gold to be mined in the very sun's red heart, where he sets over the Delphian cliffs (a gold that no thief can steal); deep-pictured tissue; impenetrable armour; potable gold. Yes; there is, there is! And it was to this fourth order of treasure that Jesus pointed in His great sermon. It was treasure of this fourth order that Mr. Little-Faith safely retained, after his robbery, in 'the place where his jewels were.' These 'the robbers never ransacked; so these he kept still.'

Now it so happened that Peter was standing by that day, and heard that great word about the robes of office that moths cannot eat, about the swords of power that rust cannot defile, and about the shining hoard that thieves cannot steal. And long afterwards the three sets of treasures were running in his mind when he himself wrote to scattered and persecuted Christians concerning the inheritance that is incorruptible, because no moth can corrupt it, and undefilable, because no rust can defile it, and unfading, because no thieves can steal it. These are the jewels that the brigands of Deadman's Lane can never touch.

Oh the night was dark and the night was late,
  And the robbers came to rob him;
And they picked the locks of his palace-gate,
  The robbers that came to rob him—
They picked the locks of his palace-gate,
Seized his jewels and gems of state,
His coffers of gold and his priceless plate,—
  The robbers that came to rob him.

But loud laughed he in the morning red!
  For of what had the robbers robbed him?
Ho! hidden safe as he slept in bed,
  When the robbers came to rob him,
They robbed him not of a golden shred
Of the radiant dreams in his wise old head—
'And they're welcome to all things else!' he said,
  When the robbers came to rob him.

The lines inevitably recall the well-known story of Jeremy Taylor. His house had been pitilessly plundered; all his choicest possessions had been squandered; his family had been turned out of doors. Yet, in face of his sore trial, the good man kneeled down and gave humble and hearty thanks to his God that his enemies had left him 'the sun and the moon, a loving wife, many friends to pity and relieve, the providence of God, all the promises of the gospel, his faith, his hope of heaven, and his charity towards his enemies!' Life's burglars and bandits can make but poor headway against a man of that temper.

But of all those whose pockets have been rifled, and whose houses have been robbed, none have suffered more heavily than Paul. He knew the skill of the robbers better than any of us. Here is his own record: 'In stripes above measure, in prisons more frequent, in deaths oft. Of the Jews five times received I forty stripes save one. Thrice was I beaten with rods, once was I stoned, thrice I suffered shipwreck, a night and a day I have been in the deep; in journeyings often, in perils of waters, in perils of robbers, in perils by mine own countrymen, in perils by the heathen, in perils in the city, in perils in the wilderness, in perils in the sea, in perils among false brethren; in weariness and painfulness, in watchings often, in hunger and thirst, in fastings often, in cold and nakedness.' Yes, 'in peril of robbers.' The sea had robbed him once, and the land had robbed him often. He knew what the robbers could steal, and he knew what they could not. 'Whether there be prophecies, they shall fail; whether there be tongues, they shall cease; whether there be knowledge, it shall vanish away.' These are life's 'spending-money,' which we may lose by violent hands in Deadman's Lane. But the apostle goes on: 'But now abideth faith, hope, love—these three; and the greatest of these is love.' These are the jewels that the robbers cannot ransack.

I had a friend,
Whose love no time could end;
That friend didst Thou to Thine own bosom take;
For this, my loss, I see no reparation;
The earth was once my home—a habitation
Of sorrow Thou hast made it for this sake.

I had a love
(This bitterest did prove);
A mystic light of joy on earth and sky;
Strange fears and hopes; a rainbow tear and smile,
A transient splendour for a little while;
Then—sudden darkness; Lord, Thou knowest why!

What have I left?
Of friend and love bereft;
Stripped bare of everything I counted dear.
What friend have I like that I lost? What call
To action? Nay, what love? Lord, I have all,
And more besides, if only Thou art near!

May this be my heart posture always let me keep my hands open to receive and for God to take.

In Florence visitors are shown the doors which Michael Angelo declared to be fit for the gates of Paradise. They are covered with exquisite pictures, and picked out with noble imagery in bronze. But those gates were once gilded, and Dante speaks of them as the 'golden gates.' The centuries have eaten away the gilt, but have been unable to touch one particle of the magnificent work of the immortal master. Let us put on a cheerful courage, therefore, as we enter Deadman's Lane. The best always abides after the gleam and the gloss have worn off.

That is for ever and for ever the strong consolation of the Christian gospel. The robbers steal the glitter; they cannot touch the gold. They take Mr. Little-Faith's spending-money; but his jewels are still his own after the brigands have decamped.

IV

'TWO—OR THREE'

A BLIND man can always tell when there is a poor congregation. In such a case the minister invariably quotes a certain text: "Where *two or three* are gathered together in My name, there am I in the midst of them.' But the text is as much out of place as the missing worshippers. We have no right to drag it in drearily, dolefully, dismally, whenever the empty pews are particularly conspicuous. It is not an apology for human absence. It is a triumphant proclamation of the divine presence. And it raises a most interesting question. Who are the TWO? And who is the possible THIRD?

'TWO—OR THREE.'

I

Who are the TWO?

Who can they be but Euodias and Syntyche, those two wrangling sisters in the church at Philippi,

and all their still more quarrelsome daughters in all
the churches of the world?   Who can they be but
Paul and Barnabas, so sharply contending; and
all their contentious sons the wide world over?
Wherever and whenever two daughters of Euodias
and Syntyche—poor ruffled creatures who have
judged rashly and spoken hastily—meet together
that they may kiss each other for Christ's dear sake,
and 'be of the same mind in the Lord,' 'there,' says
their great Master, 'am I in the midst of them.'
Wherever and whenever two sons of Paul and
Barnabas—poor inflamed disciples who have con-
tended sharply and divided suddenly—meet to-
gether that they may love each other for the gospel's
sake (until they come once more to love each other
for their own) there, says their Lord, am I in the
midst of them.   It is at such times as it is at the table
of the Lord.   There is the same real Presence, the
same thrill of the heart; the same 'thoughts that do
lie too deep for tears.' He is there, forgiving, and
teaching them the high art of forgiveness; forget-
ting, and showing them how to forget.

But the THIRD—the possible THIRD? 'Two—or
three.' Who is he? The third, if there be a third,
is clearly that blessed one of the Seventh Beatitude:
'Blessed are the peacemakers, for they shall be called
the children of God.' The possible third is some

lovely and gracious spirit who has wept in secret over the pitiful estrangement of poor thin-skinned Euodias and poor quick-tempered Syntyche. And, by her beautiful ministry, she, like an angel of peace, has brought them to this place of the Holy Presence. The possible third is some strong, sane, saintly soul who has grieved over the sharp contentions of Paul and Barnabas, and has tactfully helped them each to a discovery of the other's excellences. Where Euodias and Syntyche and such an angel meet, where Paul and Barnabas and such a Greatheart kneel, we take our shoes from off our feet, for the place whereon we stand is holy ground. It is hallowed by the Presence. 'Where two or three are gathered together in My name, there am I in the midst of them.' 'These words,' says Professor Simon, 'were spoken primarily of those who were assembled for the settlement of quarrels.' So be it.

Lydia in past Seasons

II

Who are the TWO?

Who can they be but a husband and a wife? Following upon the excellent example of Paul, Peter addresses himself to all hubsands and to all wives till wedding-bells shall chime no more. But Peter goes just one step beyond Paul, in that he

takes all his husbands and wives into his confidence,
and tells them the profound reason for his earnest
solicitude on their behalf. 'That your prayers be
not hindered,' he says. 'I have so carefully warned
and admonished and instructed you as to your atti-
tude and behaviour to each other that your prayers
be not hindered.' Happy is that bridegroom who,
when all the confetti has been thrown, when the
chattering, giggling throng is at last excluded, when
he finds himself at length alone with his bride,
kneels with her, and lays in prayer and adoration the
foundation of the new home. 'Except the Lord
build the house, they labour in vain that build it.'
Wherever and whenever a man and his wife bow in
the presence of the Highest, that they may sweeten
and strengthen and sanctify their happy union by a
common fellowship with God, there, says the
strange Guest who blessed the marriage at Cana,
there am I in the midst of them. These are the TWO.

But the THIRD—the possible THIRD? 'Two—*or
three.*' Who is he? Let us consult, in our per-
plexity, one of the fathers of the Church. Let
Clement of Alexandria tell us. 'Who are the two or
three gathered together in Christ's name, and in
whose midst the Lord is? Is it not husband and
wife *and child?*' To be sure. In the days of love's
young dream we say that 'two's company, three's

none.' But when God sends a little child into a home the early theory stands exploded, and three become company, and two become none for ever after. There is hope for Christianity so long as these three gather in His name, and He is in the midst of them. The family altar is the hub of the spiritual universe. Every husband who does not daily enjoy the benediction of the 'two or three' should straightway read the fragrant life-story of Thomas Boston. And every wife whose domestic drudgeries and social niceties are not glorified by the blessing of the 'two or three' should hasten to the nearest library for the life of Susanna Wesley. And after *he* has read the tale of Thomas Boston, and after *she* has read the story of Susanna Wesley, not a word will be said. They will rise and look into each other's faces with a glance of perfect under-standing. And 'a possible third' will be brought in from a cot or from a kitchen, and that home will be-come the gate of heaven. They will meet together, and read together, and pray together on that day and on every day that comes after it. And where those two—or three—gather together in His name, there He will be in the midst of them.

That was a great word which fell the other day from the lips of King George V: 'The foundations of national glory,' he said, 'are set in the homes of

the people. They will only remain unshaken while
the family life of our nation is strong and simple and
pure.' It was right royally spoken. Herein lies
life's wealthiest enrichment and finest fortification.

III

Who are the TWO?

Who can they be but those torch-bearers and
testifiers whom He has sent in pairs to the uttermost
ends of the earth? He sent them forth two by two,
and wherever any two of them sit by the wayside, or
kneel in the shadow, or, like the men of Emmaus,
talk as they walk, there will He be in the midst of
them. And so men have paired off ever since—Paul
and Silas, Mark and Barnabas, Luther and Melanch-
thon, Franciscan friars, Dominican monks, Lollard
preachers, Salvationist officers, travelling evan-
gelists, and a host beside. Nor are the minister and
his wife in their manse, or the missionary and his
wife at their remote outpost, any exception to the
rule. And wherever and whenever His ambassa-
dors, persecuted as Paul and Silas were persecuted,
meet together in His name, as Paul and Silas in
their prison 'prayed and sang praises unto God,'
there will He be in the midst of them, as He was
most manifestly in the midst of them on that never-

to-be-forgotten night at Philippi. It is ever so.
This great saying concerning the 'two or three' is
the watchword of the faith. It is the pledge that,
however isolated the scene, however remote the
station, however lonely the toilers, He is always
there.

But the THIRD—the possible THIRD? 'Two—*or
three.*' Who is he? Who can he be but the first
convert? Lydia, for example, that winsome soul
who, as the 'Lady of the Decoration' would have
said, 'had a beautiful big house, and a beautiful big
heart, and took us right into both.' Paul never for-
got when he and Silas and Lydia—happy three!
—met together in His name. It was the very joy
that is in the presence of the angels overflowing
into the hearts of mortal men. There was not a
shadow of doubt about it. He was clearly there in
the midst of them. Or the jailer, for example.
Paul and Silas and their jailer! What a triad! But
what a night was that! No Christian knows what
Christianity really means until he has experienced
such days as that day of Lydia's and such nights as
that night with the jailer. Religion catches fire and
becomes sensational. The moment when two weary
workers kneel with their first convert has all eternity
crammed and crowded into it. Ask Robert and
Mary Moffat if that is not so. Wherefore let every

minister and his wife, and every missionary and his wife, and every pair of Christian comrades everywhere, keep <u>an eye open day and night for the possible Number Three.</u> 'Two—*or three*,' the Master said. Three's company; two's none!

open your
hearts and
homes.

V

THE CAPTAIN OF THE SHIP

THE unvarnished fact is that even the skipper does not know everything. He sweeps the horizon with his glasses, but there are signs in the sky that elude his wary observation. He may quite easily be beaten at his own game. The seer in the cabin may decipher the language of the clouds more accurately than the bronzed and weather-beaten mariner on the quarter-deck. That was the mistake the centurion made. 'The centurion believed the master of the ship more than those things which were spoken by Paul.' It is a purely nautical matter. The captain of the ship predicts fair weather and urges an early clearance. Paul, the prisoner and passenger, foretold angry seas, and advised remaining in shelter. The centurion believed the captain of the ship. But Paul was right; the captain was wrong; and the ship was lost. Sooner or later, all life resolves itself into a desperate struggle for human credence between Paul and the captain of the ship. The point is that the captain of the ship is the man

Tension
follow
god of the
world.

who might be supposed to know. He is a specialist. And Paul sets over against his nautical erudition the unsatisfying words, 'I perceive.' It is a case of Reason on the one hand and Revelation on the other; and the centurion pins his faith to the vigilant captain rather than to the visionary Paul. That is the exact point at which the world has always missed its way. That was the trouble at the very start. Could it be that to eat of the fruit of the tree would be to die? Was it reasonable upon the face of it? And Adam believed the captain of the ship. Later Noah predicted a flood. Where were the phenomena to warrant such an alarming forecast? Did it appeal to common sense? And again the insistent voice of Revelation was scouted. Visit the melancholy sites of Edom and Babylon, of Tyre and Sidon, of Sodom and Gomorrah, of Greece and Rome, and everywhere, on crumbling pillar and broken arch, seeing eyes may discern these significant words, deeply graven on the ruins that are splendid even in decay: *They believed the captain of the ship.* These magnificent empire-builders of yesterday scouted the nebulous perceptions of the prophets, and they fell. National shipwreck always comes along that line.

It is wonderful how little the practical man really knows. A grey-headed old theorist is tapping away

Just because that's how it is, does that mean it's how it should be?

with his geological hammer among the stones and strata on the hill-side. As he leaves he remarks casually that there is coal in the mountain. The practical man smiles incredulously at the poor old fellow as he packs his hammers and glasses and specimens and strolls off home; but, a year or two later, when the hill-side is riddled with shafts, grimy with coal-dust, and black with smoke, the 'practical man' bites his lips in disgust at his failure to take the old dreamer's hint. The meteorologist shuts himself up in his laboratory among phials and chemicals. Presently he opens his door and gravely predicts a storm. The masters of the craft down at the port smile knowingly and put to sea; but when their ships are in the pitiless grip of the gale they grimly remember the forecast. Only the other day Professor Belar, Director of the Larbach Observatory, warned miners of seismic unrest that seemed likely to liberate fire-damp. He was not taken very seriously; and within a day or two all Europe stood aghast at the horror of the Lancashire colliery explosion. Paul generally knows what he is talking about.

It would be an appalling calamity if we were left at the mercy of the captain of the ship. He may be true as steel, and good as gold, but, as in the case under notice, he makes mistakes. Those who are inclined, like the centurion, to trust the captain of the ship rather than those things that are spoken by Paul will do well to consult a second captain. There are more ships than one, and the opinion of the second captain will diverge from that of the first. Doctors differ. I have recently been reading the biographies of some of our greatest English judges, and few things are more curious than the way in which two distinguished judges, equally able and equally conscientious, will hear the selfsame evidence, and listen to the selfsame speeches, and then arrive at diametrically opposite conclusions. The same phenomenon is common in politics. Great and gifted men, trained to wrestle with the problems of political economy, developing by long experience all the instincts and functions of statesmanship, will divide sharply and oppose each other hotly on the most simple issues.

Clearly the captain of the ship is unreliable. In a world like this, on which so many worlds depend, it would be the climax of misfortune if the captain of the ship had it all his own way. There are visions, perceptions, revelations. God speaks from without. He speaks plainly, so that wayfaring men may not err. Paul rises and says grandly, 'Sirs, I perceive. . . .' And that centurion is foolish indeed who believes the captain of the ship more than

Always seek counsel from a few trusted

those things that are spoken by Paul. The dusty and travel-stained pilgrims of eternity would be of all men most miserable if, amidst the babel of many advisers, no clear guidance had reached them from the haven of their desire. Happily, the Lord of the Pilgrims does not leave His Christians and Hopefuls to find the way to the Celestial City as best they may. There are the 'things spoken by Paul.'

Yet it must be admitted that there is a certain glamour and fascination about the captain of the ship. It is restful to believe him rather than to venture everything upon the verdict of a visionary. In one of the biographies to which we have referred an interesting situation occurs. It is in the Life of Sir Henry Hawkins (Baron Brampton). At the very climax of his fame as a judge, accustomed every day to weighing conflicting evidence, and deciding between opposing claims, the great judge gave himself to the study of religion, and, as a result, he joined the Roman Church. Newman's *Apologia* is a similar case. How can these 'conversions' be explained? The answer is obvious. Considered from the strictly judicial point of view of Hawkins, or from the coldly intellectual standpoint of Newman, their decisions are perfectly intelligible. They simply believed the captain of the ship. In the Roman Church they find a commander, a head, a pope. He speaks plainly, he is invested with the glamour of authority, and his decisions are final; he is the captain of the ship. But there are other voices that do not yield to such icily critical investigation. They are subtle, silent, spiritual. But they satisfy, and lead to safety. 'The centurion believed the captain of the ship more than those things which were spoken by Paul.' That is exactly what, moving along purely logical and coldly intellectual lines, Hawkins and Newman would have done.

But when all is said and done, Paul is right. A leading English minister, the other day, drew aside the veil of squalor and filth, and revealed to an eminent scientist the raw material on which he worked—the very refuse and wreckage of society. 'Is there any hope for these people?' he asked. The old professor took his time, and answered sagely, 'Pathologically speaking, there is none!' Just so. That is the verdict of the captain of the ship. But Paul cries, 'Sirs, I perceive . . . ,' and tells a vastly different tale. And which is right? Ask your ministers; ask your city missionaries; ask General Booth. Or, if you suspect these of bias, consult the works of Professor William James, the eminent psychologist, or Rider Haggard, the eminent

novelist. Professor James, in his masterpiece, con-
fessed that, in ways altogether beyond psychological
explanation, the activities of the Church have again
and again made bad men good. Spiritual energies
have wrought the most amazing moral transforma-
tions. And still more recently Rider Haggard raises
his hat in reverence before the astonishing phe-
nomenon of conversion as he has seen it for himself
in his investigations of the work of the Salvation
Army. There can be no doubt about it. The un-
seen world is the triumphant world. The spiritual
is, after all, the sane and the safe. The only way of
avoiding shipwreck in Church and in State is clearly
to pay good heed to 'the things spoken by Paul.'

VI

THE SUPREMACIES OF LIFE

LIFE has a wonderful way of tapering majestically to its climax. It narrows itself up towards its supremacies, like a mountain rising to its snow-capped summit in the skies. Our supreme interests assert themselves invincibly at the last. Our master passions are 'in at the death.' Let us glance at a pair of extraordinarily parallel illustrations.

Paul is awaiting his last appearance before Nero. The old apostle is caught and caged at last. He is writing his very last letter. He expects, if spared, to spend the winter in a Roman dungeon. 'Do your very best,' he says to Timothy, 'to come to me before winter.' 'And,' he adds, 'the cloke that I left at Troas with Carpus, when thou comest, bring with thee, and the books, but *especially the parchments*'!

Under circumstances almost exactly similar Paul's great translator, William Tyndale, was lying in his damp cell at Vilvorde awaiting the fatal stroke which set his spirit free a few weeks later. And, as in Paul's case, winter was coming on. 'Bring me,' he writes, 'a warmer cap, something to patch my leggings, a woollen shirt, and, above all, my Hebrew Bible'!

Especially the parchments!
Above all, my Hebrew Bible!

The emphasis is upon the *especially* and upon the *above all*. Paul knows how isolated he will feel in his horrid cellar, and he twice begs his young comrade to hurry to his side. He knows how cold he will be, and he pleads for his cloke. He knows how lonely will be his incarceration, and he says, 'Bring the books'! Yet he feels that, after all, these do not represent the supremacies of life. It is not on these that he is prepared to make his final stand. 'But especially the parchments'! Much as he yearns for the clasp of Timothy's hand, he is prepared, if needs be, to face the stern future alone. Much as he longs for his warm tunic to shelter his aged limbs, he is prepared, if needs be, to sit and shiver the long winter through. Gladly as he would revel in his favourite authors, he is prepared, if needs be, to sit counting the links in his chain and the stones in the wall. But the parchments! These are life's supreme, essential, indispensable requisites. These represent life's irreducible minimum. 'Espe-

cially the parchments'! 'Above all, my Hebrew
Bible'! These are the supremacies of life.

The hero of romance erects a pyramid upon its
apex. He sets out in life with one or two friends.
He soon multiplies the number. He counts them,
as the years pass, by the score and by the hundred.
And he dies at last in the possession of friendships
which can be numbered by the thousand. It is a
false note. The thing is untrue to experience. 'The
first true gentleman that ever breathed' found His
path thronged with friends at the outset. But, as
time wore on, they wore off. 'Many of His disciples
went back, and walked no more with Him.' Twelve
remained, such as they were; but even that remnant
must be sifted, and of the twelve a selection had
to be made. And into the chamber of death, and up
to the Mount of Transfiguration, and into the Gar-
den of Gethsemane 'Jesus taketh with Him Peter
and James and John.' The pyramid is narrowing
up towards its apex. And when He passes from
Gethsemane to Golgotha John alone stands by the
cross, and even he had wavered. 'And Jesus said
unto John, Son, behold thy mother.' It had tapered
sharply to the unit at last. 'Especially John.'

Sir William Robertson Nicoll has a story of an
old Scotsman who lay a-dying. His little room was
crowded with friends. Presently a number of them

rose and quietly left. There remained his old wife, Jean, and the trusted companions of a long pilgrimage. As his frame became more feeble and his eye more dim one after another reverently rose, lifted the worn old latch silently, and left the room. At last the old man pressed the withered hand in which his own was clasped, and whispered faintly: 'They will a' gang: you will stay!' And at last he and she were the sole occupants of the little chamber. 'Especially Jean.' Which things are an allegory. The pyramid narrows to its apex. Life contracts towards its supremacies. 'Especially the parchments'! 'I have hosts of friends,' wrote Lord Macaulay in one of his beautiful letters to his sister, 'but not more than half a dozen the news of whose death would spoil my breakfast.' And of that half-dozen he would probably at a later stage have made a selection. Friendship has its supremacies.

The same is, of course, true of our libraries. Like the apostle, we are all fond of books; but our bookshelves dwindle in intensity as they grow in extensity. As life goes on we accumulate more and more volumes, but we set more and more store on a few selected classics of the soul. The number of those favourites diminishes as the hair bleaches. We have a score; a dozen; and at length three. And if the hair gets very white, we find the three too

many by two. 'Especially the parchments'! Sir
H. M. Stanley set out upon his great African ex-
ploration with quite a formidable library. One can-
not march eighteen hours a day under an equatorial
sun, and he gave a prudent thought to the long en-
campments, and armed himself with books. But
books are often heavy—in a literal as well as in a
literary sense. And one by one his native servants
deserted him (the pyramid towering towards its
apex). And, as a consequence, Stanley was com-
pelled to leave one treasured set of volumes at this
African village, and another at that, until at last he
had but two books left—Shakespeare and the Bible.
And we have no doubt that, had Africa been a still
broader continent than it actually is, even Shake-
speare would have been abandoned to gratify the
curiosity of some astonished Hottentots or pigmies.
It all comes back to that pathetic entry in Lockhart's
diary at Abbotsford: 'He [Sir Walter Scott] then
desired to be wheeled through his rooms in the bath-
chair. We moved him leisurely for an hour or more
up and down the hall and the great library. "I have
seen much," he kept saying, "but nothing like my
ain hoose—give me one turn more!" Next morning
he desired to be drawn into the library and placed by
the central window, that he might look down upon
the Tweed. Here he expressed a wish that I should

read to him. I asked, from what book. He said, "Need you ask? There is but one!" I chose the fourteenth chapter of St. John's Gospel.' He listened with mild devotion, and, when Lockhart had finished reading of the Father's house and the many mansions, he said, "That is a great comfort!' The juxtaposition of phrases is arresting: 'In the *great library*'—'there is *but one book*!' The pyramid stood squarely upon its solid foundation, but it towered grandly and tapered finely towards its narrow but majestic summit. Come,' says Paul the Aged, 'for I am lonely; bring the cloke, for I am old and cold; bring the books, for my mind is hungry; but, oh, if all these fail, send the parchments!' *Especially the parchments!* Life's supremacies must always conquer and claim their own at the last.

The Bible is more than words....
It's living and active.

VII

THE PRUDENTIALITIES OF LIFE

BENEATH cloudless Italian skies Paul is painfully but patiently enduring, in a stifling cell, the suffocating fervours of the sultry summer days. And, with the fierce heat at its insufferable maximum, he casts a prudent thought ahead of him, and contemplates the severe rigours of a stern Roman winter. 'Do thy best,' he writes to Timothy, 'to come to me before winter; and the cloke which I left at Troas bring with thee.' Superficial observers have often considered these personal trivialities beneath the dignity of Scripture. The trifling is subjective; it is not objective. It is their criticism that lacks dignity. 'Eyes have they, but they see not.' The microscopic is often as eloquent and as revealing as the majestic. Divinity often trembles in a dewdrop. A trifling incident may reflect a tremendous principle. A psychologist would at least discover in the story of Paul and his summer call for his winter cloke a fine instance of the amazing detachment of which the human mind is capable. It is a strange and wonderful thing that we are able, amidst summer scenes, to project our thoughts so realistically into the coming cold that we give an involuntary shiver and cast our eyes over our wardrobes. The same power, of course, enables us to project our minds, not merely from our summer cells to our winter wardrobes, but from our own summers to other people's winters. It is by this extraordinary faculty of the mind that we sympathize. My lady, wrapped snugly in rugs and furs, detaches herself from herself, and projects herself into the wretched rags of her sister in the slums. No one can read Charles Dickens without feeling that, even as he sat in his comfortable room and wrote, he endured all the agonies of the poverty which he so passionately portrayed. Mrs. Harriet Beecher Stowe could never have written *Uncle Tom's Cabin* unless she had first projected herself, in uttermost detachment from herself, into the anguish of Cassy and Eliza. The iron entered into her own soul by this weird and awful power of intellectual abandonment. It makes even loftier flights: it explores moral territories. Lovers of *Oliver Twist* will remember how the pure, sweet girlhood of Rose Maylie came into touch with the soiled soul of poor Nancy, and for one awful moment the mind of Rose projected itself into the sins

and sorrows of Nancy; and, in the presence of that
marvel, Nancy burst into tears. 'O, lady, lady!'
she cried, clasping her hands passionately before her
face, 'if there were more like *you,* there would be
fewer like *me*—there would, there would!' And,
travelling along this road, we should soon come to
that culminating example of mental and moral de-
tachment by which the redemption of a lost world
was effected. From the summer-time of His glory
and holiness He detached Himself from Himself—
emptied Himself—and wept with us in the winter of
our raggedness and shame. 'He had compassion'!
The ages can know no greater miracle or mystery
than that.

But the purely psychological phenomenon pre-
sented by Paul's summer call for his winter cloke has
led us a little astray. A wayfaring man will recog-
nize it as an illustration of the prudentialities of life.
Paul anticipates in summer the demands of winter.
Such prudentialities are everywhere. The great
mountain heights store up in winter their millions
upon millions of tons of snow; and when early sum-
mer suns have dried up the lower springs, and when
otherwise the plains would be scorched beneath a
pitiless glare, the welcome streams come flowing
down from the heights, and the grateful cattle
quench their thirst. In the same way, the soft green

mosses along the banks of the rivulet saturate themselves with moisture like sponges, conserving and protecting it, and in the later days of drought, when else the bed of the stream would be dry, they release their precious burthen, and the thirsty bless them. In animate creatures the faculty is, of course, much more pronounced. Everybody knows how ants and beetles make elaborate preparations for days as yet far ahead of them. The mice and the squirrels make hay while the sun shines, and lay up in store against frost and snow. The bee provides her honey when the earth is gay with flowers with the intention of living upon her hoard when no blossoms are to be seen. We remember reading in Parkman's *Conspiracy of Pontiac,* of the folly of the Algonquin Indian who, 'in the hour of plenty, forgets the season of want,' until, 'stiff and stark, with haggard cheek and shrivelled lip, he lies among the snowdrifts; till, with tooth and claw the famished wild cat strives in vain to pierce the frigid marble of his limbs.' There is a more excellent way. And Paul, following the example of mice and squirrels and bees, thinks of winter cold while as yet he perspires beneath summer suns. The most obvious application of the principle is, naturally, the most practical one. Those who are too dense to catch our meaning had better inquire for an interpretation of it at a savings bank, a building society, or an insurance office. It is true, of course, that, concerning many things, to-morrow must not obtrude upon to-day; but the future has its certainties, and it would be both impious and absurd to neglect them. Since it is certain that winter must follow summer, it is certain that it is the duty of Paul to arrange for his cloke. A man must provide for his home whilst as yet he is single; he must make his will whilst in the best of health—the applications are simply innumerable. But the truth has its deeper aspects. In the heyday of spiritual prosperity we must lay up in store against days of darkness and doubt. In the days of opened heavens and answered prayers let us record the experience on the tablets of memory, to feed upon when the heavens are as brass and prayer as a tinkling cymbal. 'When infidel thoughts come knocking at my door,' wrote good old Thomas Shepard, 'I send them away with this answer: Why should I question that truth which I have both seen and known in better days?' There is a world of sagacity and shrewdness there!

It was an awful night in Scotland. The snow was deep; the wind simply shrieked around the little hut in which a good old elder lay dying. His daughter brought the family Bible to his bedside.

'Father,' she said, 'will I read a chapter to ye?'

But the old man was in sore pain, and only moaned. She opened the book.

'Na, na, lassie,' he said, 'the storm's up noo; I theekit [thatched] my hoose in the calm weather!'

We can learn no loftier philosophy than that from the story of Paul's summer call for his winter cloke. We must thatch our houses in the calm weather, and, later on, smile at the storm. Life's truest prudentiality lies just there!

VIII

THE FACE AT THE WINDOW

WE are living in a very wistful world. It is all very well to say that people are irreligious, callous, indifferent. That is true; but it is not the whole of the truth. When Mr. H. G. Wells' *First Men in the Moon* reached their lunar destination the moon seemed to them to be lifeless, derelict, desolate; but when they probed beneath the surface they found it teeming with pulsing life, and furious thought, and industrial activity. And the more deeply they penetrated into its cavernous tunnels and mysterious subways the more populous the place became. Which is, as Mr. Wells very possibly meant it to be, an allegory. [It is when we look with superficial eyes upon the world that we are pessimists. When we scratch the surface we begin to behold the truth.] One of those noble and graceful Hebrew metaphors which, for sheer literary beauty, have never been surpassed, reflects most perfectly the whole position. 'My soul doth wait for the Lord more than they that watch for the morning; I say, *more than they that*

watch for the morning.' The image is one of ex-
quisite tenderness and pathos. The night is long
and dreary, and the tired watchers press their faces
every now and then against the window-pane, eager
to discover beyond the rugged ranges some grey
glimmer of the coming dawn. The soul of many a
man has its eastward aspect. There are great num-
bers who dwell in chambers like that in which Chris-
tian was lodged in the Palace Beautiful, 'whose
window opened *toward the sun-rising.'* The soul of
the psalmist is in the darkness, but his face is to-
wards the dawn. We are in grave peril, in our
pessimistic moods, of forgetting the face at the
window. It is the essential feature in the present
situation. There are pilgrims 'asking the way to
Zion with their faces thitherward.'

Let my meaning mirror itself in a pair of illustra-
tions. Here are two such faces peering wistfully
out from the dark.

The first is that of Frank T. Bullen. In *With
Christ at Sea,* he says, 'Arriving in Sydney, I soon
succeeded in getting a berth as lamp-trimmer in one
of the coasting steamers, and for the next twelve
months made a pretty complete circuit of the Aus-
tralasian colonies, living on the best of everything,
earning good wages, learning all manner of things
harmful to me, but never by any chance coming

across any one who was Christianly disposed, and feeling myself less and less anxious to seek after God. Often I would stand on deck, when anchored in Sydney Harbour on Sunday morning, and listen to the church bells playing 'Sicilian Mariners,' *with a dull ache at my heart, a deep longing for something, I knew not what.'* Thus ends the quotation; but the tragic fact is that there were excellent people, with Bibles and hymn-books, passing along the quay on the way to church, who glanced at the grimy young lamp-trimmer and thought him irreligious, callous, and indifferent! They failed to see the wistful face at the window.

The other occurs in the memoir of Dr. H. Grattan Guinness. On one of the earliest pages we read: 'Never shall I forget one evening, when the ship was anchored in a calm off Lowestoft, near Yarmouth, looking at the sun slowly setting in the west over the peaceful scene, the outline of a church spire rising among trees showing distinctly against the glowing sky. I was *longing unutterably* to be permitted to dwell in some quiet spot where, out of the reach of evil society and the voice of blasphemy, I might worship God and walk with Him in unhindered fellowship.'

'Longing unutterably!' 'More than they that watch for the morning.' That is it!

The fact is that we are too superficial. We glance at a man and at once tie an imaginary label round his neck. We classify him as a Christian, or as a heretic, or as a sceptic, or as a backslider; and we think that *that* settles it. But our work of classification is very much more complicated than we think. We forget that a saint and a sceptic can dwell together in the same skin. *Lord, I believe*—there you have the saint! *Help Thou mine unbelief*—there you have the sceptic! The prophets loved to talk of a time when the wolf should lie down with the lamb; but in many a heart the wolf and the lamb dwell together even now. Great wickedness and great wistfulness often lodge in the self-same heart. The room may be very dark indeed, but the face is at the window looking towards the light. We are slow to learn the lesson that Robert Louis Stevenson tried to teach us in his allegory of Dr. Jekyll and Mr. Hyde. As the years go by we learn to economize our labels.

Dr. Campbell Morgan was recently asked by an interviewer for his view of the spiritual condition of London. 'On the one hand,' he replied, 'I see evidence of awful indifference, but on the other I see remarkable wistfulness. I find that, when I get into touch with the most indifferent men, there is a great wistfulness that was absent a few years ago.

The man who then told me that he was an agnostic
still says that he is an agnostic, but he adds now
that he dearly wishes he could believe as I do.' That
testimony is significant. It means that the men who
sit in thick darkness are moving towards the window
and longing for the dawn.

Dr. Douglas Adam has told us a striking story of
Professor Huxley. 'A friend of mine,' says Dr.
Adam, 'was acting on a Royal Commission of which
Professor Huxley was a member. One Sunday he
and the great scientist were staying in a little coun-
try town. "I suppose you are going to church," said
Huxley. "Yes," replied the friend. "What if, in-
stead, you stayed at home and talked to me of your
religion?" "No," was the reply, "for I am not clever
enough to refute your arguments." "But what if
you simply told me of your own experience—what
religion has done for you?" My friend did not go
to church that morning. He stayed at home and told
Huxley the story of all that Christ had been to him.
And presently there were tears in the eyes of the
great agnostic as he said, "I would give my right
hand if I could believe that!" ' Huxley's face was
at the window, in spite of everything.

But, of course, the peerless illustration of our
point is the infinitely pathetic case of Professor
Sidgwick. Has any minister ever read that life-

story with dry eyes? If so, we are sorry for his congregation. To enter into the cheerless realm of Sidgwick's scepticism is a more chilling experience than to penetrate polar solitudes. And yet no one can read that throbbing story without seeing a tear-stained face at the window. Long and wistfully the brilliant doctor strained his eyes, looking eastward, but saw not the roseate flush of the dawn. He felt, through it all, that his doubt was his shame; and his soul ached for faith. He literally longed for the light 'more than they that watch for the morning; I say, more than they that watch for the morning.' There was unbelief in his brain, but a wonderful wistfulness shone in his yearning eyes. Beneath his intellectual uncertainties he carried a pitifully hungry heart. Others such as Mill and Tyndall, Professor Clifford and Viscount Amberley might, of course, easily be cited to swell this cloud of witnesses; but there is no need.

Let us, however, before laying aside the pen, cross the ocean in order to inquire whether this strange and wistful craving is confined to grimy lamp-trimmers like Frank Bullen, and to brilliant University professors like Henry Sidgwick; or is it to be discovered also in the regions beyond? And so soon as we step ashore it becomes manifest that, without an exception, the peoples who sit in darkness have, nevertheless, their faces to the window. In every land 'there be many that say, Who will show us any good?' On continents and on islands blind souls are everywhere groping after the light. It must be so. If, as Principal Iverach argues in his *Christian Message,* the Founder of Christianity be in very deed the Son of God, it is inconceivable that the human heart can find its home in Mohammedanism or Buddhism. Only recently a great All-India Convention of Religions was held at Allahabad. Hinduism, Islamism, Jainism, Zoroastrianism, Judaism, and Theosophy were all strongly represented. But it was agreed, by general consent, that the only message that 'struck warm' was the witness of the Indian Christians to the love and power of Christ. To that testimony a sympathetic chord of response vibrated in all hearts. And, at the close of the Convention, the Hindu secretary exclaimed, 'The one thing we could not have dispensed with was the Christian contribution!' It was like a streak of dawn streaming in upon the tired watchers of the night. 'The Lady of the Decoration' tells us that she saw in Japan 'a wistfulness that I have never seen anywhere else, except in the eyes of a dog.' The letters of our missionaries on every field often remind us of that unforgettable cartoon which appeared in *Punch* in the dark days of 1885. It repre-

sented General Gordon on the roof of his palace
at Khartoum, shading his eager eyes with his hand
and gazing with a look of unutterable wistfulness
towards the sandy horizon, watching for that reliev-
ing column that ultimately came too late. He waited
for their coming more than they that watch for the
morning. So do the nations.

> Sudden, before my inward open vision,
>   Millions of faces crowded up to view,
> Sad eyes that said: 'For us is no provision,
>   Give us your Saviour, too!
>
> 'Give us,' they cry, 'your cup of consolation;
>   Never to our outreaching hands 'tis passed;
> We long for the Desire of every nation,
>   And, oh, we die so fast!'

These are the faces at the window. When little
Bilney made his historic confession to Hugh
Latimer, which lit that candle in England that has
never been put out, an image akin to this haunted
his imagination. 'Oh, Father Latimer,' he said,
'prithee, hear me: when I read in the Latin Testa-
ment of the great Erasmus these strange words—
"Christ Jesus came into the world to save sinners,"
it was with me as though in the midst of a dark
night, *day suddenly broke!*' That is the daybreak
for which the faces watch at the windows of the

world 'more than they that watch for the morning;
I say, more than they that watch for the morning.'
The exquisite winsomeness of the Christian evangel
and the wondrous wistfulness of a waiting world
are the two strong pillars on which we build our
serene confidence in the day after to-morrow.

IX

BACK MOVES

I was enjoying the rare blessedness of an evening free from engagements. I was revelling in the luxury of a glorious arm-chair, a blazing fire, and a fascinating book. The children were seated at the table behind me, absorbed in the desperate hazards of the game that lay between them. The only noise was the rustle of the leaves of my book. But at length the silence was broken. 'You can't do that!' I heard one of the players cry, 'there are *no back moves!*' I read on; but had not gone far when I came upon this sentence: 'The unseen opponent in the great game of life, while scrupulously fair, will allow *no back moves,* and makes us pay in full for every blunder.' The words, of course, are Huxley's. I wonder if he is right! I am not at all sure that he has spoken the last word.

So many men find their lives entangled, prejudiced, compromised, that unless you can promise them something in the nature of a back move the most you can offer seems so paltry and small. Go to an almshouse, for example, and the old people will remind you that you can't give them their lives over again. Visit a jail, and, in some form or other, the terrible question will present itself in every cell: 'Can I begin again at the point at which I went astray?' Talk to a man who is in the grip of the drink fiend. He does not doubt for a moment the willingness of God to forgive. He is even inclined to think it possible that the power of God might be able to keep him from the dreadful snare. But see the stain on his life! He thinks with unspeakable horror of his tarnished name, his humiliated wife, his trembling hand. Have you nothing to say to him about a fresh start, a clean sheet, a back move? If not, you will lose him in spite of everything.

Now I imagine that most of us have passed through three distinct phases of thought on this subject. I confess that I have. They are three inevitable stages of development. First of all, there was the period at which we assured men, with the most sublime confidence, that their sins, like a dark cloud, could be blotted from the face of the sky and wiped into oblivion. The ugly stain, we told them, could be perfectly and eternally erased. We boasted, in our fine evangelistic fervour, that a sinner might not only be pardoned, but be justified. For a sinful man to be justified, we elaborately explained, was for a wicked man to be made as though he had never been wicked at all. Sin is not only forgiven; it is annihilated, cast behind God's back, hurled into the depths of the sea. Salvation, under that first interpretation, was nothing less than a magnificent back move.

Then came doubts, suspicions, and the *second* phase. We found it was not all so simple as we thought. The jail-bird is converted; but who will trust him? The old record is so damning! The drunkard kneels in a tempest of tears at the penitent-form; but the bloated face, and the palsied hand, and —worse still—the awful craving are there still. We recalled John B. Gough's bitter, bitter cry: 'The scars remain!' he lamented, 'scars never to be eradicated, never to be removed in this life. I have been plucked like a brand from the burning; but the scar of the fire is on me!' And George Mac Donald emphasizes, with a very tender but a very telling touch, another aspect of the same problem. The passage occurs in *Wilfrid Cumbermede*. 'Do you know, Wilfrid, I once shot a little bird—for no good, but just to shoot at something. I knew it was wrong, yet I drew the trigger. It dropped, a heap of ruffled feathers. I shall never get that little bird out of my head. And the worst of it is that, to all eternity I can never make any atonement.' 'But

God will forgive you, Charley!' 'What do I care
for that,' he rejoined almost fiercely, 'when *the little
bird cannot forgive me?*' Yes, there is just that
element in life that makes back moves very difficult.
And, unhappily, the wreckage men have wrought
is not always confined to a heap of ruffled feathers.
What if, whilst Heaven absolves, earth finds it hard
to entertain kind thoughts of us? What if, instead
of little birds, our own flesh and blood rise up in
judgment against us? There is, undoubtedly, a
good deal to give pause to our early theology; a
good deal to enforce the cheerless philosophy of
Omar Khayyám:

> The Moving Finger writes; and, having writ,
> Moves on: nor all your piety nor wit
>   Shall lure it back to cancel half a line,
> Nor all your tears wash out a word of it.

We abode among these sombre thoughts for many
years, and fancied that we had reached finality. We
pitched our tent in this dismal wilderness and re-
garded it as home. We foolishly imagined that this
was the last phase, and that there was no more to
be said. And when the felon looked eagerly up into
our eyes, as he sat in his lonely cell, and asked about
the new start, the clean sheet, the back move, we
were dumb.

Then came emancipation, and the third phase. And, as usual, the Bible brought it. We were browsing among the prophecies; we came upon Jeremiah's story of the potter. 'Then I went down to the potter's house, and, behold, he wrought a work on the wheels. And the vessel that he made of clay was marred in the hand of the potter: so *he made it again* another vessel, as seemed good to the potter to make it. Then the word of the Lord came to me saying, O house of Israel, cannot I do with you as this potter? saith the Lord.' *He made it again!* That is surely as near to a *back move* as it is possible to get! I remember hearing the Rev. F. B. Meyer tell of a woman who, on her way to commit suicide, heard the singing in Christ Church, Westminster, and stole into the porch. She was only a poor, soiled, broken bit of London's outcast womanhood. It happened that Mr. Meyer preached on the story of the potter, the vessel marred and remade. There was no further thought of suicide. She was charmed at the prospect of a back move. Surely when Jesus talked to Nicodemus of being 'born again,' He was promising a back move!

Then, too, in turning over these ancient prophecies, I came to Joel. Everybody knows that the entire prophecy of Joel was suggested by the historic and unprecedented plague of locusts which had

just devastated the entire land. The very sun was
darkened, the fields and vineyards were a howling
wilderness, business in the city was paralysed;
even the sacrifices in the Temple were suspended.
In the midst of this awful visitation, this fearful
scourge, this national calamity, the prophet was
commanded to cry: 'Fear not, O land; be glad and
rejoice: for the Lord will do great things. I will
restore to you the years that the locust hath eaten.'
And the promise, royally given, was royally fulfilled.
The sun was once more shining out of a clear sky.
The vines were bowing beneath the burden of
wealthy and luscious clusters. The hills, with rich,
delicious grass for the cattle, were as green as
emerald. The valleys laughed and sang with their
golden crops of corn. The city was humming with
commercial prosperity. And, to crown all, the
temple was once again crowded with devout wor-
shippers. The years that the locust had eaten were
all fully restored.

Now if only I could go to that felon's cell, to
that drunkard's home, and to a hundred other places
that occur to me, with a message like that! 'I
will restore to you the years that the locust hath
eaten!' That would be grand! That would be a
gospel of back moves with a vengeance! And may
I not? Now let me think!

Life stopped

God does His for us too

How was the promise fulfilled? *How* did the Most High restore the years that the locust had eaten? It is very simple. What the locusts took, they took; and there was no return. But the next year? Why, the next year the hills and valleys of Palestine were such a scene of abundant harvest and prodigal growth that the people were fully compensated for the loss of the previous season. Now, as the children say, we are getting warm!

Have we never known a life that, in its later years, displayed a sweetness and a purity and a grace which were the direct outcome of earlier suffering or of earlier sin? Can we not recall the memory of saintly and fruitful lives in which both the sanctity and the fruitfulness were the natural result of hideous memories of former transgression? It was the haunting nightmare of their old sins that drove both Bunyan and Newton to such intense personal piety and to such fervent evangelistic zeal. We have all known men who, in days gone by, lived in open and notorious shame. Then came the change. Their faith was a pattern to us all in its exquisite and childlike simplicity. The very enormity of their transgressions made religion a revelry to them and the thought of pardon a perpetual luxury. Their faces were radiant. They never referred to their experiences but with stream-

ing eyes and faltering voices. Their testimony was
so impressive as to carry conviction to all who heard
it. And as we saw how strong men were moved by
their utterance we felt that God, in His own wise
and wonderful way, was restoring to them the years
that the locust had eaten. In the familiar lines of
Hezekiah Butterworth there are two significant *buts*,
and we are in danger of noticing only the one:

> *But* the bird with the broken pinion
>   Never soared so high again.

This is the first. That is the truth that Huxley saw.
But it is not the whole truth. There is another
but:

> *But* the bird with the broken pinion
>   Kept another from the snare,
> And the life that sin had stricken
>   Raised another from despair.
> Each loss has its compensations,
>   There is healing for every pain;
> Though the bird with the broken pinion
>   Never soars so high again.

Life may be different but we do heal.

And, surely, surely, to 'save another from the snare,'
or to 'raise another from despair' is the very best of
back moves! 'I do not regret the past,' cried the
'Lady of the Decoration,' at the close of her story,
'for through it the present *is*. All the loneliness, the

heartaches, and the pains are justified now! I believe that, whilst I have been struggling out here in Japan, God has restored to me the years that the locust had eaten, and that I shall be permitted to return to a new life, a life given back by God!' Who shall say that life has no *back moves* after that?

X

THE TIRELESS TRUDGE

WHILST the fire crackled cheerily between them two friends of mine discussed a knotty point. The question under debate was, briefly, this: Which is the most trying part of a long journey? One argued for the initial steps on setting out. The weary road, he said, stretches out interminably before you. Every stick and stone seems to be shouting at you to turn back and to take your ease. His friend, on the other side of the hearth, thought quite differently. He contended stoutly for the final stage of the pilgrimage. He vividly pictured the exhausted pedestrian at the end of his journey, scarcely able to drag one blistered and bleeding foot in front of the other. It is certainly rather a fine point; but, after all, it was really not worth discussing, for nothing is more absolutely clear than that they were both wrong. Which, of course, is the usual fate of controversialists.

Now the worst part of a journey is neither at its beginning nor at its close. There is a certain in-

70

It's about the issue not each other.

describable exhilaration arising from the making of
the effort which imparts elasticity to the muscles and
courage to the mind, at starting. The road seems
to dare and challenge the pilgrim, and he swings off
along the taunting trail with a keen relish and a
buoyant stride. And, at the other end, the twinkling
lights of the city that he seeks help him to forget
that he is footsore and choked with the dust of the
road. His blood tingles with the triumph of his
achievement and the delight of nearing his goal.
But there is *another* stage concerning which neither
of my friends had a word to say. What of the
intermediate stage? What of the long and lonely
tramp? What of the hours through which no
applauding voices from behind can encourage and
no familiar fingers from before can beckon? This,
surely, is the worst part of the way! There is no
intellectual stimulant so intoxicating as the forma-
tion of a noble purpose, the conception of a sudden
resolve, the making of a great decision. And, in the
luxurious revelry of that stimulus the prodigal finds
it easy to rise from the degradations of the far coun-
try and to fling himself with a will along the great
Phoenician road. And at the other end! Surely
the most overpowering of all human instincts and
emotions is that which holds captive every nerve at
the dear sight of home! No; neither the first nor

[margin, handwritten: Ambition that has not been beaten down]

[margin, handwritten: Victory]

the last steps of that familiar journey were very hard to take. But between the one and the other! What questionings and forebodings! What haltings and backward glances! What doubts and fears! Yes, there can be no doubt about it, both my friends were wrong.

It is the intermediate stage that tests the mettle of the man. It is the long, fatiguing trudge out of sight of both starting-point and destination that puts the heaviest strain on heart and brain. That is precisely what Isaiah meant in the best known and most quoted of all his prophecies. He promises that, on the return from Babylon to Jerusalem, 'they that wait upon the Lord shall renew their strength; they shall mount up with wings as eagles; they shall run, and not be weary; *and they shall walk, and not faint.'* Israel is to be released at last from her long captivity. Imagine the departure from Babylon—its fond anticipations, its rapturous ecstasies, its delirious transports! Those first steps of the journey were not trying; they were more like flying. The delighted people walked with winged feet. And the last steps—with Jerusalem actually in sight, the pilgrims actually climbing the mountains that surrounded the holy and beautiful city—what rush of noble and tender emotions would expel and banish all thought of weariness! But

Isaiah is thinking of the long, long tramp between
—the drag across the desert, and the march all void
of music. It is with this terrible test in mind that
he utters his heartening promise: 'They shall walk
and not faint.' They would fly, as on wings of
eagles, out of Babylon at the beginning; they would
run, forgetful of fatigue, into Jerusalem at the
end; but they should *walk* and not faint. That is
life's crowning comfort. The very climax of divine
grace is the grace that nerves us for the least
romantic stage of the journey. Farewells and wel-
comes, departures and arrivals, have adjusting com-
pensations peculiar to themselves; but it is the glory
of the gospel that it has something to say to the
lonely traveller on the dusty tract. Religion draws
nearer when romance deserts. Grace holds on when
the gilt wears off.

Two cases come to mind. I know a man whose
whole delight was in his boy—a little fellow of six
or so. Then, suddenly, like lamps blown out by a
sudden gust, the lad's eyes failed him, and he was
blind. The father was the recipient of scores of
touchingly sympathetic letters. All sorts of people
called. Kindly references were made in press and
pulpit. The man had no idea until that moment that
he had so many friends. All the world seemed to
be paying homage to his sorrow. *That* was the be-

ginning. After many years the boy had been taught to interpret the world again by means of his remaining senses. There was nothing he could not do. He earned his own living, and his sightlessness seemed no real hindrance to him. *That* was the end. But the father told me that the strain of it all came between these two. There came a time when the postman brought no cheering letters. Friends uttered no heartening words. The world had transferred his boy's blindness into the realm of the normal and the commonplace. Nobody noticed. But in the home the little fellow staggered about, and his parents' hearts ached for him. What was to become of him? It was during those intervening years lying between the first crushing blow and the final relief that the real strain came. That was by far the worst stretch of the road.

I knew a woman. Without a moment's warning she was plunged into widowhood, and left to battle for her five little children and herself. There was an extraordinary outburst of affectionate sympathy on the part of all who knew her. Then came the funeral. After that the world went on its way again as though nothing had happened. *That* was the beginning. After the years, the battle had been well fought and well won. The children had been clothed, educated, and placed in positions of usefulness and honour. *That* was the end. But my widowed friend told me that *she* did not forget when the world forgot. Every morning her grief woke up with her. And every night it followed her to her rest. Every day, as she struggled for her little ones, the haunting question tortured her: What would become of them if sickness or death seized upon her? That was the killing time. That intermediate stretch was the worst part of the desolate way.

As it is with individuals, so it is with great causes. A crusade is launched amidst vituperation, derision, and execration. And there is enough fight in most of us to lend a certain enjoyment to the very bitterness of antagonism. And at last the self-same movement is crowned with triumph. But the real inwardness of the struggle lies midway. William Wilberforce used to say that he was less dismayed by the storm that broke upon him when first he pleaded the cause of the slave than by the 'long lull' that followed when the country accepted his principles, but did nothing to hasten their realization. In America the same thing happened. The war against slavery was undertaken with a light heart. Young men sprang to the front in thousands with the refrain of 'John Brown's body' on their lips. But the real struggle was not then, nor towards the close, when victory and emancipation were in sight. But who can forget the long agony of disaster that intervened between those two? It was when the nation was trudging tearfully along that blood-marked track that the real suffering took place. The same experience repeats itself in the history of every great reform. Some one has said that every movement has its *bow-wow* stage, its *pooh-pooh* stage, and its *hear-hear* stage. Of those three phases the central one is infinitely the most difficult to negotiate. Between the howl of execration that greets the suggestion of a reform and the shout of applause that announces its final triumph there is a long and tiresome stretch of steep and stony road that is very hard to tread. They are God's heroes who set a stout heart to that stiff brae, and walk and *not faint*.

In his *Autobiography* Mark Rutherford tells of his fierce struggle with the drink fiend. On one never-to-be-forgotten night he resolutely put the glass from him and went to bed having drunk nothing but water. 'But,' he continues, 'the struggle was not felt just then. It came later, when the first enthusiasm of a new purpose had faded away.' And, in his *Deliverance* he applies the same principle in a more general way. He is telling of the stress of his life as a whole. 'Neither the first nor the last,' he says, 'has been the difficult step with me, but rather *what lies between.* The first is usually helped by the excitement and promise of new beginnings, and the last by the prospect of triumph. But the intermediate path is unassisted by enthusiasm, and it is here we are so likely to faint.' I cannot close more fittingly than by setting those two striking sentences over against each other: 'It is here we are *so likely to faint,*' says Mark Rutherford, speaking of the long and tiresome intermediate phase. 'They shall walk *and not faint,*' says the prophet in reference to precisely the same circumstances and conditions. Wherefore let all those who are feeling the toilsome drudgery of the long and unromantic trail pay good heed to such comfortable words.

XI

SUNSET ON THE SEA

'UNCLE TOM and Eva were seated on a little mossy seat in an arbour at the foot of the garden. It was Sunday evening, and Eva's Bible lay open on her knee. She read: "And I saw *a sea of glass, mingled with fire.*" "Tom," said Eva, suddenly stopping and pointing to the lake, "there 'tis!" "What, Miss Eva?" "Don't you see?—there," said the child, pointing to the glassy water, which, as it rose and fell, reflected the golden glow of the sky. "There's *a sea of glass, mingled with fire.*" '

The exegesis of Mrs. Stowe's frail little heroine is probably as near the truth as our best expositors are likely to carry us. I have known what it is to be surrounded by magnificent and mountainous icebergs in the Southern Ocean; I have been an awe-stricken admirer of the grandeur of a thunder-storm on the equator; I have seen the seas in a passion as they responded to a gale off Cape Horn; but I must confess that one of the most splendid and impressive spectacles it has ever been my lot to witness was a tropical sunset at sea. The huge and angry sun went down like a ball of livid fire. The sky seemed to have broken into flame. The sea was a sea of blood. The very foam on the tips of the waves was tinged with crimson. The outlook from the deck of the vessel was unforgettable—the kind of thing to haunt you in your dreams. Everything was weird, awful, unearthly. And as I gazed upon the strange mingling of flood and flame I thought of John. The exiled apostle sat among the beetling cliffs of Patmos after having borne the burden and heat of the toilsome convict day. And at evening he gazed wearily and wistfully westwards towards those teeming centres of civilization into which he had hoped to carry the story of the Cross. And, even as he gazed, the cold Aegean Sea flamed with the glory of an Oriental sunset; and he beheld at his feet 'a sea of glass, mingled with fire.'

The fact is that the seeming antagonisms of life are not so incongruous as we, in our superficial moments, are apt to suppose. We are in imminent peril of reaching false conclusions through taking it for granted that the other side of truth is always a lie. We forget that fire and water are in greater concord than we assume. Truth consists not in a part, but in the whole; and the separate parts of that whole are often apparently inconsistent. Professor Henry Drummond has shown us that the 'time was when the science of geology was inter-preted exclusively in terms of the action of a single force—*fire*. Then followed the theories of an opposing school, who saw all the earth's formations to be the result of *water*. Any biology, any soci-ology, any evolution,' adds the professor, 'which is based on a single factor is as untrue as the old geology.' Geologians never approximated to the real truth until they saw 'a sea of glass, mingled with fire.' And from those ancient blunders of the geologians, our theologians, if they be discreet, may still learn much. Knowledge is not the mono-poly of any one of her numerous schools.

The fact is that Truth is always and everywhere friendly to Truth. It therefore follows, as the night the day, that Truth need never be afraid of Truth. One man may interpret Truth in the terms of a sea of glass; another may interpret Truth in the terms of a flame of fire. A superficial hearer, listening to the two interpretations, will throw up his hands in horror. 'Babel and confusion!' he will cry. 'Which is true and which is false?' But a wise man will listen reverently to both preachers, and will see that a sea of glass may quite easily, and quite naturally, be mingled with fire. A few years ago there awoke in Europe a spirit of scientific research. The geologist took his hammer and began to search among the strata for truth. The astronomer swept the heavens with his telescope in his quest of truth. The antiquarian and historian went off together to the East with a spade, and began to dig in Palestine, Egypt, Asia Minor, and Assyria for truth. And there were excellent souls in all the churches who cried for mercy. 'Stop!' they cried, 'you will find something among stones or stars that will stagger our faith or shatter our serenity. You will dig up something in some lone Syrian town that will contradict our Bibles!' But Science would not stop. Investigation and scrutiny hastened forward. And with what result? We see now that, whilst Science appeared to our grandsires like a sea of glass, as compared with Revelation, which was like a flame of fire, the two are not contradictory or antagonistic. They harmonize and blend. And we to-day see 'a sea of glass, mingled with fire.'

It is the glory of the Christian faith that it is immense enough to be able to contain within itself aspects and elements that at first sight seem strangely conflicting. I heard a preacher exulting in the tenderness and beauty of God's infinite love. The very same day I heard another speak of the severity and exactness of God's infinite justice. Surely he was speaking of a different God! But no; it is the same God, but *such* a God! There is no conflict nor confusion. We are simply gazing at a sea of glass, mingled with fire. He is 'a just God *and* a Saviour.' And those who know Him and worship Him are like unto Him. Dean Stanley has a most exquisite passage, in which he extols these diverse qualities in the life of Arnold. He describes the perfect ease and delicacy with which Arnold revelled in the atmosphere of the home. Those who had only seen the stern schoolmaster in the halls of Rugby scarcely recognized him as he romped with the merry children by the hearth. And those who had only known him in the home, a man so engaging, so winsome, so delightful, listened as to a strange language when others referred to his strictness and austerity. 'Yet,' says Stanley, 'both were perfectly natural to him; the severity and the playfulness expressing, each in its turn, the earnestness with which he entered into the business of life, and the enjoyment with which he entered into its rest.' In a word, his character, which was perhaps more reverenced than that of any man of his time, was like 'a sea of glass, mingled with fire.'

The splendour of the sunset on the sea has a very practical application to the testimony and teaching of all the Christian churches. Let us take, by way of illustration, two extreme cases. I repeat that both instances are necessarily—and happily—extreme. A fine church, splendidly upholstered and appointed, but only moderately attended. Its pulpit is regarded as the last word in scholarship—and that is as it should be. But it is said to be 'cold.' The ministry is forbidding; the atmosphere lacks cordiality. On the way home the worshippers are arrested by a spectacle so remote from that from which they have just departed that they might almost mistake it for a representation of a different religion. A street preacher screams and yells in a frenzied monotone. His theology is almost brutal; his illustrations are shocking; his gesticulation is terrifying; his grammar causes even the children to smile. But his arresting passion, his grim earnestness, his transparent sincerity, his vivid realization of the awful realities of which he speaks—these are beyond question.

If only the other preacher had caught something of his intensity, and if only he had taken the pains to acquire something of that preacher's erudition, what scenes might have been witnessed both from the cushioned pew and from the corner of the pavement! As it is, both are largely ineffective. The one is like the sea—*deep, but cold.* The other is like the sun—*blazing, but wearying.* The seer at Patmos saw that the ideal lies, not in the lowering

of the scholarship of the one, nor in the reduction
of the fervour of the other, but in the mingling of
the two—'a sea of glass, mingled with fire.' The
problem is not one of subtraction, but of addition.
It is said that young men sometimes enter theo-
logical seminaries overflowing, like *volcanoes*, with
fires of enthusiasm that they can neither hide nor
contain. And it is said, too, that they frequently
emerge from those colleges like *icebergs*—very im-
pressive, but very cold. It is usually their own fault
when such moral tragedies occur. At least, it is a
thousand shames things should so fall out. The
youthful fires ought to be fed and purified by the
addition of knowledge. The minister, as he waves
farewell to his Alma Mater, should carry with him
his youthful ardour absolutely undiminished and
unabated, with all his scholastic acquirements as a
clear addition.

Of all the rites and ordinances of Christian wor-
ship the same may be said. Our services and
assemblies are intended to be seas of glass, mingled
with fire. Solemnity must be there, and dignity;
but there must be emotion and deep feeling as well.
Splendid music must be shot through with spiritual
praise. Stately eloquence must be glorified by stir-
ring passion. All the externals and ceremonials of
worship are in themselves as cold as icicles. The

most beautiful and impressive ordinances are simply seas of glass till they are mingled with fire. It is only as they are made luminous with intense spiritual significance that they reveal their glory to the eyes of men. Nothing is more flat, stale, and unprofitable than an argument concerning the mere technicalities and externals of an ordinance. Yet nothing is more inflaming to all that is best within us than the actual commemoration of these lovely rites. Baptism, apart from the profound spiritual sanctions with which the Scriptures invest it, is a sea of glass. But with the realization of those inner mysteries and experiences, the waters flame and burn. Paul tells us that the same is true of the Lord's Supper. 'He that eateth and drinketh unworthily, eateth and drinketh damnation to himself, *not discerning the Lord's body.*' To such a one, that is to say, the elements are dumb; the waters do not glow with fire. He sees the sea, but not the sun. Little Eva and Uncle Tom were, therefore, unconsciously embarking on a voyage amidst the eternal verities as they gazed upon the sunlit lake at New Orleans on that beauteous and tranquil Sunday evening. And we shall be permanently enriched if we catch something of the radiant significance of the vision that they saw. Our seas and suns—our floods and flames—must mingle.

PART II

PART II

CLEAN BOWLED!

THERE is something wonderfully restful to the eye, and strangely soothing to the mind, about the very environment of a first-class cricket-match. The green and tented field, fanned by the balmy breath of summer and fragrant with the peculiar but pleasant odour of the turf; the huge stands, musical with the hum of eager conversation and the ripple of easy laughter; the dash of colour imparted by gay dresses, fluttering flags, and the creamy flannels of the players; and, last but not least, the immense crowd, garrulous with reminiscences of earlier contests and overflowing with geniality and good temper. And then, crowning all, the glorious game itself! Harold Begbie does well to lilt its praise:

England has played at many a game, and ever her toy was a ball;
But the meadow game, with the beautiful name, is king and lord of them all.
Cricket is king and lord of them all, through the sweet green English shires;
And here's to the bat and the ball (How's that?), and the heart that never tires.

Nothing is more certain than that a recreation which holds the devoted attachment of a great people must, in the very nature of things, be preeminently a matter of morals. In his monumental work, *The Rise of the Dutch Republic,* John Lothrop Motley says that 'from the amusements of a people may be gathered much that is necessary for a proper estimation of its character.' And he proceeds to demonstrate, with his wonted insight and sagacity, the truth of this general proposition from the experience of that sturdy little people whose most distinguished historian he must for ever remain. Goethe, too, that profound yet practical philosopher, has laid it down 'that men show their character in nothing more clearly than by what they think laughable.' And Macaulay, in paying tribute to Frederick of Rheinsberg, remarks that 'perhaps more light is thrown on his character by what passed during his hours of relaxation than by his battles or his laws.' The evidence of three such witnesses— Motley, Goethe, and Macaulay—must be regarded as indisputable. One has only to think of the gladiators and martyrs who were 'butchered to make a Roman holiday,' and to remind oneself that five thousand horses and twelve hundred bulls are annually slaughtered in Spanish bull-rings, to see that Paganism on the one hand, and Popery on the other,

betray their characters in the very recreations of
their devotees. From a gladiatorial combat in
ancient Rome or a bull-fight in modern Madrid to a
test cricket-match in England or Australia is a far,
far cry. The question inevitably arises: What has
made the difference? There is only one answer
possible. It is *the Cross*! It is not too much to
claim that the gospel of Jesus Christ has trans-
figured and softened and beautified the very sports
and pastimes of those who have come beneath its
charm.

But the thing that has most impressed me, as I
have watched these splendid contests, is the startling
suddenness with which calamity swoops down upon
a player, and imports a new atmosphere into the
game. A man may bat most brilliantly for half a
day. You watch him hour after hour. He blocks
and cuts and pulls and drives with a consistency
that becomes almost monotonous. Bowler after
bowler is tried, but their task seems hopeless. Then
—a dog yelps behind you. You turn your head to
see what is amiss, and in that fraction of a second
there is a click and a cry and a cheer. And as
you look hastily back to the field, you see the
scattered stumps; and the hero of the hours is setting
out from the crease to the pavilion. Before you
turned your head you actually saw the bowler com-

mence his delivery. He did not wave his hand and
cry, '*This* is the ball that is going to do it!' The
men in the field gave no signal. The batsman
looked as he had looked for hours. There was
absolutely nothing to lead you to suspect that the
fatal ball was actually leaving the bowler's hands.
So suddenly, swiftly, sensationally—like a bolt from
the blue—calamity pounces down upon a man, and
there is no place for repentance though he seeks it
earnestly with tears. The broken wicket is irrepar-
able. He may explain and excuse, but he cannot
return.

I have been reading Mr. Stewart E. White's *The
Forest.* It is a most entrancing description of travel
with the Indians among the woods and waterways
of North America. And it contains, among other
fine things, a splendid chapter on 'Canoeing.' He
says, *inter alia,* that 'in a four-hour run across an
open bay you will encounter somewhat over a thou-
sand waves, no two of which are exactly alike, and
any one of which can swamp you only too easily if
it is not correctly met.' Each wave, he tells us, has
an individuality of its own. It requires a poise and
a balance and a movement quite distinct from those
demanded by any other wave. And he adds: *Re-
member this: be just as careful with the very last
wave as you were with the others. Get inside before*

you draw that deep breath of relief. That sentence is
sage, striking, significant. It seems to matter very
little whether you are canoeing in America or
cricketing in Australia; the same principle is at
work. In the one case, the waves seem all alike;
yet each wave has its own peculiar peril, and the
Indian who, for one little second, is off his guard
finds himself wallowing in the surging torrent. In
the other case, the balls seem all alike; yet each has
a trick of its own, and the unhappy batsman who,
for one instant, plays mechanically or carelessly is
rudely recalled by the hideous rattle of the wrecked
wicket behind him. In canoeing and in cricketing
disaster leaps upon its astonished victim with such
sensational swiftness.

'In canoeing and in cricketing.' And in every-
thing else for that matter. That is a trite and
terrible verse of George MacDonald's:

> 'Alas, how easily things go wrong!
> A sigh too deep, or a kiss too long;
> And then comes a mist and a weeping rain,
> And life is never the same again.

That is it. Life, for most of us, is wonderfully
like the experience of the Australian batsman and
the American boatman. It is very strenuous and
full of peril. Every nerve is taut. Each wave and

each ball must be negotiated as though all destinies
hung trembling on our triumph over that particular
wave, our mastery of that particular ball. Most of
us can recall pathetic instances of crushing moral
disaster. Their very memory casts a heavy gloom
over our spirits still. Our idols fell, and we remem-
ber the shock and the stagger. 'Who can see worse
days,' asks Bacon, 'than he that, yet living, doth fol-
low at the funeral of his own reputation?' It is
absolutely the last word in human tragedy and sor-
row. Yet how fearfully swiftly it all happened! .
The thunder-bolt pounced out of a cloudless sky
and stupefied us by its appalling suddenness. The
morning of that moral shipwreck broke as calmly
as any since the world began. The sun shone just
as brightly; the birds sang just as blithely; the
flowers bloomed just as sweetly; and all the world
was fair. It was like the fatal ball and the fatal
wave. There was nothing about that day to dis-
tinguish it from any other day. Yet that day, in an
unwary moment, the gust of temptation did what
many storms had failed to do. The hero fell. In
giving evidence at the memorable Tay Bridge in-
quiry in Scotland, Admiral Dougall attributed the
collapse of the great bridge to a sudden pressure of
wind from an unaccustomed quarter. 'Even trees,'
he added, 'are not able to resist pressure from un-

usual directions. A tree spreads out its roots in the
direction of the prevailing wind.' The moral is
obvious.

I find my hand trembling as I write. My peril
is so intensely real and so terribly acute. I may
bat for hours and pile up the centuries upon the scor-
ingboard; and then, in the twinkling of an eye, a
ball with a slightly different break may astonish me
by compassing my downfall. I may battle for hours
with the racing and foam-tipped breakers; and
then, as suddenly as a lightning flash, a wave of
innocent appearance but of peculiar peril may wreck
my frail little craft within sight and sound of home.
A gust of temptation from an unusual quarter may
work for me such havoc as the sudden squall did for
the famous Scottish bridge. Wherefore, says Mr.
Stewart E. White, 'Remember this: be just as care-
ful with the very last wave as you were with the
others. Get *inside* before you draw that deep breath
of relief.' And a still greater and even more experi-
enced traveller adds: 'Let him that thinketh he
standeth take heed lest he fall.' The logic of the
flying bails is irresistible. And it is so wofully easy
to be *caught in the slips.*

II

MAD DOGS AND MOSQUITOES

I ENTERED a chemist's shop. The polite apothecary asked me to wait awhile, and, to save my soul from the tedium of staring vacantly at his immense coloured bottles, he very kindly handed me a copy of a magazine. It proved to be the current number of *The British Importer.* It did not appear promising; it was scarcely in my line; the chances of a thrill seemed remote. I fancied that the coloured bottles might be more exciting, after all. But I suddenly revised my judgment. The word WARNING! caught my eye. It was at the top of a reproduction of a card issued by the Incorporated Liverpool School of Tropical Medicine. It bore the signatures of the Princess Christian, the Earl of Derby, Lord Cromer, and a host of other distinguished individuals. It proclaimed as its object that it aimed at the prevention of Climatic Fever, Malaria, Yellow Fever, Dengue Fever, Coast Fever, Endemical Fever, Remittent Fever, and Bilious Re-

mittent Fever—a truly terrible array.   And it laid
down, as an indisputable proposition,

*That the Bite of a Mosquito should be dreaded as
much as that of a Mad Dog.*

I thanked her Royal Highness, I expressed my
obligations to these noble lords and learned doctors
for so interesting a statement so concisely phrased,
and, laying aside *The British Importer,* from which
I had imported as much as I could carry in one load,
I gave myself furiously to think.

The fact is, of course, that the mad dog has gone
out of fashion.   He had his vogue, and it was a
great one while it lasted.   But his day is dead.   The
turn of the mosquito has come.   It is perhaps a
little disconcerting and a little humiliating, but it is
irresistibly true.   And, since it is so resistlessly true,
it is better to face the facts.   In his magnificent
History of the Nineteenth Century Mr. Robert Mc-
Kenzie broke the news to us as gently as he could.
That great chapter on 'The Redress of Wrongs,'
which haunts the ear for ever like a shout of
triumph, might have been entitled: 'The Slaughter
of the Mad Dogs.'   I very respectfully present the
suggestion to Mr. McKenzie, with an eye to future
editions.   In that stately chapter he marshals the

hideous injustices and social tyrannies under which men groaned but a generation or two ago. He recites, in glowing language, the glorious story of reform. And when he has told his thrilling tale, and has described the destruction of one monstrous evil after another, he brings his chapter to a conclusion with a sentence that you learn by heart, simply because you cannot help it. 'The injustice of ages has been cancelled,' he cries triumphantly; 'the Hampdens of the future must be contented to occupy themselves mainly with the correction of small and uninteresting evils.' The mad dogs are all slain, that is to say; the reformers of to-morrow must turn their attention, like the Princess and the peers whose proclamation set me scribbling, to the matter of the mosquitoes.

In his *Heretics* Mr. G. K. Chesterton scented this truth of the mad dogs and the mosquitoes, but distantly. He describes what he calls the war between the telescope and the microscope. Compared with this, he thinks, the war between Russia and Japan is but a storm in a teacup. In the past we have abandoned ourselves to the worship of bigness. We have strutted about the planet looking for big things, and the natural result is that we have found them all. Now what is to be done? The telescope is of no further use. And it's far too early to go to bed.

Out with the microscope! Make the stones tell their story. Let the leaf of every tree, and the wing of every fly, and the petal of every flower unfold their lovely tales. A fig for the telescope! Its pleasures are so easily exhausted. Hurrah for the microscope! Its domain is without limit; its future is eternal. There are at least a million million mosquitoes for every mad dog. Then who cares for mad dogs? Let's get to the mosquitoes!

Many years ago a singular custom prevailed in addressing children. The good man would look into the eyes of his youthful auditors, and, assuming a melodramatic tone, intended to convey the idea that he was about to impart something sensational, he would say: 'Peradventure, my boys, I am even now addressing some future Columbus or Captain Cook, some Polar explorer or celebrated discoverer!' And in those olden times the argument was very effective; but it has, of course, been blown to bits since then. The last time it was used, one of the boys asked permission to submit a question. 'What's the good of being a Christopher Columbus,' he asked, 'now that you have no more Americas to be discovered? What's the good of being a Captain Cook now that we've seen pictures of every rock and reef that pokes its head out of the ocean? What's the good of being a Polar explorer when there are no

more Poles?' That is the point. We cannot be ex-
pected to supply new Africas for every budding
Livingstone, new Mexicos for every prospective
Cortes; and the supply of Poles is certainly shock-
ingly limited. What then? Shall we put the
shutters up? Not at all.

When Major Leonard Darwin delivered his presi-
dential address to the Royal Geographical Society,
this matter of mad dogs and mosquitoes was evi-
dently at the back of his mind. 'It is true,' he said,
'that the South Pole is as yet uncaptured, that the
map of Arabia is still largely composed of great
blank spaces, and that the bend of the Brahmaputra
is drawn by guesswork in our atlases. But it is
probable that all these problems will be solved
almost immediately. What, then, is there left for
the Royal Geographical Society to do? The So-
ciety must, then, direct its efforts with more per-
sistence than heretofore in the direction of encourag-
ing travellers to make detailed and systematic ex-
aminations of comparatively small areas.' Bravely
said! 'The mad dogs are nearly all slaughtered,'
the learned President seems to say. 'Gentlemen of
the Royal Geographical Society, let us turn our at-
tention to the mosquitoes!' 'The Hampdens of the
future must be contented to occupy themselves
mainly with the correction of small and uninterest-

ing evils.' Exit—the mad dog! Enter—the mosquito!

> Wouldst thou be a hero? Wait not then supinely
>   For fields of fine romance that no day brings;
> The finest work oft lies in doing finely
>   A multitude of unromantic things!

But we must probe more deeply yet. The greatest word ever spoken about mad dogs and mosquitoes was uttered by Paul. He always seems to have the last word about everything. 'We wrestle,' he says, 'not against flesh and blood, but against spiritual wickedness.' Our fiercest fight, he tells us, is not with the coarse sins of the flesh—mad dogs—but with sins that are as insidious and ubiquitous and invisible as mosquitoes in the night. And, as our Princess and peers have told us, 'the bite of a mosquito is as much to be dreaded as that of a mad dog.' 'If,' says old William Law, 'we would make any real progress in religion, we must not only abhor gross and notorious sins, but we must regulate the innocent and lawful parts of our behaviour and put the most common and allowed actions of life under the rules of discretion and piety.' That is precisely Paul's point.

But by this time my reader can think of no one but Thomas Chalmers and his early ministry at Kilmany. How he thundered at the mad dogs! He preached against adultery and robbery and murder twice every Sabbath. But, as he himself confessed, no good ever came of it. Then came the memorable illness and his wonderful conversion. Every minister ought to give his people that great page of Scotland's spiritual history in Chalmers' own beautiful but billowy language. And after his conversion the mad dogs troubled Chalmers no more. We hear no more about sensuality—about what Paul calls 'flesh and blood.' But, instead, we hear a great deal of a multitude of microscopic pests, of which we heard no single word before. He laments his impetuosity; he deplores his being 'bustled'; he weeps over his coldness. 'Oh my sinful emulations!' he cries; 'my ambition of superiority over others! my lack of meekness! my want of purity of heart. My heart is overspread with thorns.' Here, too, is a record of a terrific tussle with a mosquito. 'Had asked John Bonthorn to supper yesternight,' he says in his diary, 'and told him with emphasis that we supped at *nine*. He came this night at *eight*. All forbearance and civility left me, and with my prayers I mixed the darkness of that heart which hateth his brother. This is most truly lamentable, and reveals to me the exceeding nakedness of my heart.'

Yes, there is no doubt about it. These princes
of the holier life—Paul, and Law, and Chalmers—
know what they are talking about. Our real conflict
is not with the mad dogs, but with the mosquitoes.

Hear two witnesses. Professor Momerie asks:
'Will you say that the man who has made your
home a very hell by his morose and sullen temper is
more righteous than the man who has stolen your
handkerchief? Why, the misery caused by all the
pickpockets in the world to the whole human race
is less than that inflicted on your single self by the
so-called little sins of your relative's detestable
temper.' In his lovely essay on Charles Lamb, the
Right Hon. Augustine Birrell, M.P., confesses that
the gentle Elia was too fond of gin and water. But
he asks if 'an occasional intoxication which hurt no
one but himself' is to be considered a more damning
offence than the pale jealousy, the speckled malice,
the boundless self-conceit, the maddening petulance,
and the spiteful ill-will of others, who, though they
lifted no glass to their lips, broke many hearts by
their bitterness and envy? We find it hard to an-
swer these questions of the learned professor and
the distinguished statesman. But this much is clear:
it is all a matter of mad dogs and mosquitoes.

A young lady asked Charles Dickens to enter his
confessions in her album. 'What is your pet aver-

sion?' one question ran.   To which Dickens replied,
'Having the calves of my legs gnawed off by a mad
dog!' The experience is certainly not alluring; but,
then, how many people have endured it? and how
many have been tortured by mosquitoes?   Mad
dogs have slain their hundreds, but mosquitoes have
slain their tens of thousands.   For the venom of
these tiny creatures is fearfully fatal.   As witness
the long list of fevers mentioned in the proclama-
tion of the Princess and the peers, and attributed by
them to the ubiquitous mosquito.   Or ask Paul, or
Law, or Chalmers, or the man whose face you see
daily in the mirror.   Wherefore, as the proclama-
tion puts it, 'the bite of a mosquito should be
dreaded as much as that of a mad dog.'   The card
bears the title, *A warning to wise men.*   That is
very suggestive; there is no more to be said.

III

ON FALLING IN LOVE

I AM attracted to my present theme by the merest freak of circumstance. I was shown a most interesting letter. As I read that letter I felt as one might feel who is suddenly transported to Mexico or Tibet. Everything was absolutely foreign to me. The language was unfamiliar, and the atmosphere was one which I had never breathed. As a matter of fact, it 'was the letter of an accomplished pianist concerning music and musicians. The writer lives, moves, and has her being in a world which, I blush to confess, I have never invaded. A message from Mars could not have possessed greater novelty. But let me hasten to the point. The writer speaks of her acquaintance with a certain eminent pianist whose recitals crowd the most spacious auditoriums in Europe with ecstatic admirers. But, our correspondent goes on to say, there is just one thing lacking. This brilliant pianist is a lonely, taciturn man, and a certain coldness and aloofness steal into his play. And then the writer of our letter mentions the name of a lady pianist. That

name is a household word in musical circles the wide
world over; and the writer says that, to her per-
sonal knowledge, this illustrious lady one day laid
her hand on the shoulder of the brilliant young
performer, and said: 'Will you let me tell you, my
boy, that your playing lacks one thing. So far you
have missed the greatest thing in the world. And,
unless you fall in love, there will always be a certain
cold perfection about your music. Unless you come
to love another human being passionately and un-
selfishly, you will never touch human hearts as
deeply as you might.'

Now I have confessed that when I read the letter
in the presence of the person to whom it was ad-
dressed, I felt myself a pilgrim in a foreign clime,
as much abroad as an Esquimaux in Italy. But
even an Esquimaux in Italy would at least be inter-
ested, would look about and stare if he did not
understand. I found myself similarly arrested.
Then, becoming sceptical, I turned to the recipient
of the letter and asked him if a very liberal dis-
count might not reasonably be deducted in con-
sideration of the pardonable enthusiasm and ex-
cusable exaggeration of so attached a musical
devotee? Did not imagination count for some-
thing? 'Well,' replied he, 'the singular thing is that
the writer of the letter was a pupil of the illustrious

lady pianist to whom she refers. One day, at the conclusion of a lesson, the pupil looked up into the face of her teacher and told her that she had a secret to reveal. 'I know you have,' replied the instructor, 'although it is no secret.' The girl told of her engagement. 'Yes,' answered the teacher, 'but it is not quite new; it is some time ago!' 'That is so, but however did you know?' 'I noticed the difference in your playing at once, and I have observed the change ever since. I was wondering when you were going to tell me!'

I am still a stranger in a strange land. The flowers wear strange hues; the birds are of unfamiliar plumage and of unaccustomed song; I do not understand the ways of the people; I cannot speak their language; I am all abroad, and hopelessly lost. But I have been here long enough to satisfy myself that, strange as it all is, the country is a real country. The things at which I marvel are real things. I am not being tricked by a mirage. It is no illusion; I do not dream.

It is worth thinking about, partly because the same sort of thing is to be met with in other realms than in that of music. It is not merely that love lends to life a new interest, a new rapture, or even a new outlook. Everybody recalls the lines of Tennyson's 'Lover':

Let no one ask me how it came to pass,
  It seems that I am happy, that for me
'A greener emerald twinkles in the grass,
  A bluer sapphire melts into the sea.

But the suggestion in the letter that lies before
me goes further than that. It means, if it means
anything, that love liberates powers which before
were simply latent. An Arctic explorer has re-
cently drawn our attention to a most singular phe-
nomenon. He tells us that some years ago a party
of British sailors landed on an isle in the frozen
North, and, by some mischance, set fire to the
stunted vegetation that scantily clothed the inhospi-
table place. They left it a bare and blackened rock.
A few years later another party landed and found
it clothed with a forest of silver birch-trees, with
stems that glittered in the sunlight and leaves that
quivered in the wind. It was a scene of sylvan love-
liness. The flames had awakened slumbering seeds
which, in the cruel grip of the icy cold, had lain
dormant throughout the years. The wilderness had
blossomed like the rose. Now the letter suggests
that, when the soul of a man is stirred and swept
by life's most masterful passion, new and unsus-
pected powers spring into activity and fruition.

Two instances leap to mind. I suppose Scottish
literature holds no lovelier gem than the famous

letter of Dr. John Brown to Dr. John Cairns. It is
printed in *Rab and his Friends*. In that letter Dr.
Brown tells the pathetic story of Dr. Belfrage. Dr.
Belfrage's wife was a lady of great sweetness and
delicacy. After less than a year of singular and
unbroken happiness, she suddenly died. The doctor
was disconsolate, and his grief was intensified by the
reflection that there existed no portrait of his lost
love. He resolved that there should be one. He
had not an idea of painting. He had never touched
an easel. He went to the nearest art emporium,
procured all the necessary materials, shut himself
up in unbroken solitude for fourteen days, and at
the end of that time emerged from his seclusion
bearing a portrait of his late bride which became the
admiration of all who were privileged to behold it.
'I do not know of anything,' says Dr. Brown, 'more
remarkable in the history of human sorrow and
resolve.'

The other case is, of course, that of Quintin
Matsys. He was a Flemish blacksmith. He be-
came deeply enamoured of the daughter of a painter;
but the painter had vowed that his daughter should
marry none but a distinguished master of his own
craft. Matsys laid down his hammer and left the
forge; he entered a studio, and seized the brush.
And to-day—four centuries after his death—pil-

grims and tourists cross Europe to gaze upon the
mystery of his 'Descent from the Cross' in Ant-
werp Cathedral, and his 'Two Misers' at Windsor.
Ella Wheeler Wilcox, with her usual subtlety and
discernment, has sung to us in a similar strain:

Though critics may bow to art, and I am its own true
    lover,
It is not Art, but Heart, which wins the wide world over.
Though perfect the player's touch, little if any he sways us,
Unless we feel his heart throb through the music he plays
    us.
It is not the artist's skill which into our souls comes steal-
    ing,
With a joy that is almost pain, but it is the player's feeling.

I have thought—though I hesitate to say it—that
all this may explain a mystery otherwise incapable
of solution. I speak as to wise men. Many of us
are teachers, officers, ministers, and the like. We
are frequently confronted with doleful cries and still
more doleful facts. Here are articles on 'The
Dearth of Conversions,' and here are plaintive
papers on 'The Arrested Progress of the Church.'
Has my theme nothing to do with it? I fancy it has.
May not the ministry of the preacher, like the
music of the player, lack that subtle element of pas-
sion that makes just all the difference? I fancy I
detect in my own ministry sometimes—I will not

dare to speak of the work of others—that very self-same 'coldness and aloofness' which the lack of love explained in the distinguished pianist. 'Though I speak with the tongues of men and of angels, and have not love, I am become as sounding brass and a tinkling cymbal.' It is a very old complaint, but none the less tragic on that account. We take it for granted that we preach Christ because we love Christ; but *is the assumption always safe?* May we not rather cry, with Tennyson's poor fallen queen?—

> Ah, my God,
> What might I not have made of Thy fair world
> Had I but loved Thy highest creature here?
> It was my duty to have loved the highest!

'The more I love Christ,' exclaimed Gustave Doré, 'the better I can paint Him!' Of course! The most accomplished, the most biblical, the most evangelical ministry may, after all, resemble the playing of our European professor—'an indescribable coldness, a strange aloofness'—one thing lacking. There can be no doubt that Love exercises singular influences and wields potent charms. *'Had I but loved!'* cries poor Queen Guinevere in the anguish of her remorse. But no minister or teacher can afford to risk the visitation of that most poignant and pitiful regret.

IV

IPECACUANHA

IN his scathing criticism of Bertrand Barère, Macaulay tells us that the subject of his strictures was a man who employed 'phrases in which orators of his class delight, and which, on all men who have the smallest insight into politics, produce an effect very similar to that of ipecacuanha.' I am afraid that, if the expressive condemnation which the historian thus sheeted home upon the world of politics were to be aimed in the direction of the Christian Church, she could not, without some equivocation, resist the dread impeachment. There is a classical Scripture example of the same phenomenon. Thousands of years ago a tortured soul sat patiently listening to the painful platitudes of his would-be comforters. They endeavoured to propound to him the significance of the afflictions by which he was overwhelmed. And when the last echo of the philosophy of Eliphaz had trembled away into silence, poor Job found himself impressed with nothing so much as with its utter insipidity. And it was then that he sighed out his immortal question: 'Is there any taste in the white of an egg?' The discourse to which he had listened had 'produced an effect very similar to that of ipecacuanha.'

But that was in the days when the world was very young and men knew very little. Yet the same thing happens every day. Sir J. R. Seeley says, in *Ecce Homo*, that the sin which Christ most vigorously denounced is the sin to which the modern Church is most prone—the sin of insipidity. The pious commonplaces with which we glibly attempt to solace the suffering are often pathetically tasteless. The man whose darling hopes have been cruelly shattered is told, with a serene smile and an upward glance, that 'it might have been worse.' The man whose heart is bleeding, and worse than broken, is reminded that 'these things cannot be helped.' We indolently surmise that 'it is all for the best.' Tennyson tells us of the pallid consolations which were offered him in that awful hour when the man with whom his soul was knit was snatched away to a premature grave:

> One writes that 'Other friends remain,'
> That 'loss is common to the race';
> And common is the commonplace,
> And vacant chaff well meant for grain.

That loss is common does not make
My own less bitter, rather more;
Too common! Never morning wore
To evening but some heart did break.

In other words, the poet asked: Is there any taste
in the white of an egg? The comfort was insipid,
tasteless; it produced an effect very similar to that
of *ipecacuanha*!

Now, quite obviously, here is an evil thing and a
bitter. We have no right to play with crushed
spirits and breaking hearts. 'A man in distress,'
says John Foster, 'has peculiarly a right not to be
trifled with by the application of unadapted ex-
pedients; since insufficient consolations but mock
him, and deceptive consolations betray him.' I re-
member very vividly a circumstance of my child-
hood. It was my first introduction to the problem
of human loss, and it profoundly affected me. I
chanced to be standing, on a sunny afternoon, by
the gates of the local infirmary. It was visiting day.
As I watched the relatives arriving I was struck
with the appearance of a big, brawny man from the
country. He made no secret of his excitement. He
had evidently counted the hours, and had spruced
himself up like a village bridegroom for the occa-
sion. He approached the porter: 'I've come to see
my wife, Martha Jennings,' he said. The porter

consulted a book, and then, with what seemed to be brutal abruptness, replied: *'Martha Jennings is dead!'* I saw the bronzed face blanch; I saw the strong man stagger. I watched him as he clung to the iron palings for support, and bowed himself in a passion of weeping. And then, as I stood there, good-natured people, pitying, essayed to comfort him. They rang the changes on the commonplaces. 'Other friends remain!' 'Loss is common to the race!' But it was of no use: 'All vacant chaff well meant for grain.' It produced an effect very similar to that of ipecacuanha! I have never entered the chamber of death in all the years of my ministry without recalling the tragedy I witnessed that Sunday afternoon.

Now, in the cases before us, what was wrong? *This* was wrong. In all these platitudes that were tossed to Tennyson and to my friend at the hospital yesterday, and to Job the day before, four vital aspects of suffering were overlooked.

1. Our commonplaces of comfort are insipid because they ignored the *illuminative* aspect of anguish. We forget the flood of light that streams from the Cross and that has transfigured tears for ever. Such frigid philosophy as that which we have quoted can be found in Marcus Aurelius, in Plato, and in all the stoical philosophers. And in them it

is pardonable, even admirable. But from those who live in the light, better things are hoped. Christ has come! And from His disciples the weeping sons of sorrow expect, not the stone that would have been flung them by the Platonic schoolmaster, but the bread and wine of the kingdom of heaven.

2. The insipidity of our consolations often arises from the fact that we ignore the *purgatorial* aspect of pain. As though the torments of his body were not enough, Eliphaz tortured the soul of Job by telling him that purity and pain were incompatible, and that his suffering was the result of his sin. 'Who ever suffered being innocent?' he stupidly asks. It is the philosophy of the pessimist. It relates all suffering to a black, black past as *penal*. But the theology of the optimist relates all suffering to a bright, bright future as *purgatorial*. Poor Eliphaz did not know, but we ought not to forget that a lamb which was ever the emblem of innocence has become also the symbol of suffering. If the doctrine of Eliphaz were sound, the sufferer can only grin and bear it. But it is not sound. And therefore the New Testament selects, as its word for suffering, the great word 'tribulation,' which reminds us of the 'tribulum,' the threshing-machine whose work is not to punish the wheat, but to sift it. The fires of God

are never to devour, but ever to refine. It was because Eliphaz failed to remind Job of this that his hearers found the sermon so tedious. It made him cry, as with Hamlet:

> O God! O God!
> How weary, stale, flat, and unprofitable!

It produced an effect very similar to that of *ipecacuanha*!

3. The insipidity is always manifest when the *sacrificial* aspect of suffering is ignored. There is a sense in which every sob is a sacrament. The sign of the Cross is stamped on all human anguish. You suffer for my good, and I bear sorrow for yours. Dickens unfolds this wonderful secret in *David Copperfield*. Mrs. Gummidge is the most self-centred, ill-content, cross-grained woman in Yarmouth. Then comes the angel of sorrow. All those around her are plunged in the shadow of a terrible calamity. And, in ministering to them, the whole life and character of Mrs. Gummidge was transfigured. David stood in amazement before the strange and beautiful transformation.

> If none were sick and none were sad,
>   What service could we render?
> I think if we were always glad,
>   We scarcely could be tender.

Did our beloved never need
  Our patient ministration,
Earth would grow cold, and miss, indeed,
  Its sweetest consolation.

If sorrow never claimed our heart,
  And every wish were granted,
Patience would die, and hope depart—
  Life would be disenchanted.

4. And the insipidity of our consolations often arises from their neglect of the *positive* or *possessive* aspect of human loss. Whatever has been swept away in the terrible cataclysm, the best always remains. In Lord Beaconsfield's great novel he tells how Coningsby, in bemoaning the loss of his fortune, is suddenly reminded that he still possesses his limbs. In *The Scapegoat* Hall Caine tells how Israel left his little blind and deaf and dumb daughter Naomi, and wandered through the wilderness of this world. And he saw a slave-girl sold in the market-place, and he thanked God that his Naomi was free. And he heard the girl curse her father, and he thanked God for the deep love of poor little Naomi. And he saw a poor little girl that was a lunatic, and he thanked God that Naomi had her reason clear. And then the great deprivations of Naomi seemed swallowed up in the treasures that she still possessed. As Mrs. Browning sings:

All are not taken; there are left behind
Living Beloveds, tender looks to bring,
And make the daylight still a happy thing,
And tender voices to make soft the wind.

That is a great sentence of two words that the Mohammedan always engraves on the tombstones of his departed: *God remains!* Let us but cast these four ingredients into the chalice of comfort that we are preparing for the quivering lips of our weeping friends, and, so far from it producing an effect that shall resemble ipecacuanha, it shall seem to them as bracing and invigorating as the new wine of the kingdom of heaven.

V

SEASIDE LODGINGS

I AM writing on a hot Australian summer afternoon. The children are at home from school. The cities are sultry and stifling. The delicious seclusion of the fields and the refreshing cool of the seaside beckon us away. The bush and the beach call loudly. And even the solitudes seem to feel that their time has come. The wilderness blossoms like the rose. Settlements that all through the winter have been dreary desolations of mud and monotony become transformed into fairylands of poetry and romance. The great bush silences are broken by shouts of merriment and peals of laughter. Columns of smoke curl upwards, and bear witness to picnics and camp-fires. Boats dart in and out of every quiet creek and cove. Birds that have twittered and piped on dripping boughs throughout the winter without an audience are frightened hither and thither by a rush of white blouses and straw hats. It is all very refreshing and very delightful. But, with the return of the holiday season, comes back the old problem of seaside lodgings and holiday accommodation. Which reminds me.

Lovers of Mark Rutherford—and the number includes all who know him—will never forget Mary Mardon. She casts her tender spell over every fascinating page. And not least among her charms is her description of her visit, with her father, to the seaside. 'The railway station was in a disagreeable part of the town, and when we came out we walked along a dismal row of very plain-looking houses. There were cards in the window with "Lodgings" written on them, and father wanted to go in and ask the terms. I said I did not wish to stay in such a dull street, but father could not afford to pay for a sea-view, and so we went in to inquire. We then found that what we thought were the *fronts* of the houses were the *backs,* and that the *fronts faced the bay.* They had pretty gardens on the other side, and *a glorious, sunny prospect over the ocean.'*

So much for Mark Rutherford and Mary Mardon. I fancy this kind of thing is more common than we often think. The lodgings from which we eventually obtain our loveliest views are frequently rather forbidding than prepossessing. They ban rather than beckon. We dub those dwellings dull from whose windows we afterwards catch glimpses of radiant glory.

For the most obvious application of this homely truth we need not go beyond the delightful characters whom we have already introduced. Turn back a few pages to Mark's first meeting with Mary. Whilst he debated vigorously with her father she sat silently by. He mentally accused her of intellectual paucity, of possessing a small mind, and of a stupid inability to discuss important themes. He looked upon her exactly as she had looked upon the repulsive houses by the seaside. But he was as utterly mistaken as was she. It turned out that she was being tortured that evening by a maddening neuralgia. He then penitently reflected that, had such anguish been his, he would have let all the world know of it. And, he says, 'thinking about Mary as I walked home, I perceived that her ability to be quiet, to subdue herself, to resist for a whole evening the temptation to draw attention to herself by telling us what she was enduring, was heroism, and that my contrary tendency was pitiful vanity. I perceived that such virtues as patience and self-denial—which, clad in russet dress, I had often passed by unnoticed when I had found them amongst the poor or the humble—were more precious and more ennobling to their possessor than poetic yearnings or the power to propound rhetorically to the world my grievances or agonies.' This experience of Mark Rutherford in relation to Mary Mardon is clearly the precise social counterpart of her own experience in relation to the seaside lodgings. And later on, as every reader knows, she gave to him, as the lodgings gave to her, many a glorious outlook upon the infinite and the sublime.

All this is, of course, true of the Church. The men of Jerusalem looked up at the spacious and splendid proportions of the Temple. It was a stately pile of quarried stone. That was the *outside* view. But those who were permitted to stand amidst the awful sanctities of the Most Holy Place saw that, *within*, all was of finest gold. It is a parable. Readers of Bunyan's immortal allegory must have noticed that the illustrious dreamer took no pains to give an attractive impression of the exterior of the Palace Beautiful. But, like the king's daughter, it was 'all glorious within.' And notice this: 'When the morning was up they had Christian to the top of the palace, and bid him look south. And, behold, at a great distance, he saw a most pleasant, mountainous country, beautified with woods, vineyards, fruits of all sorts, flowers also, with springs, and fountains, very delectable to behold. Then he asked the name of the country; they said it was IMMANUEL'S LAND.'

We have no word to say in disparagement of those who devote their best efforts to the attempt to render the Church attractive and alluring. But we venture to suspect that their most strenuous exertions will never meet with more than a very moderate success. After you have insisted, and rightly insisted, that there should be no oratory to compare with pulpit oratory, and no music that can hold its own beside church music, you have still to admit that, so long as the Church sternly adheres to that spiritual programme for which alone she stands, she will always appear, like Mary Mardon's seaside lodgings, somewhat forbidding and repellent. Christian worship is too exquisitely modest for gaudy display. Sin, righteousness, and judgement are not themes that lend themselves to merriment. There is nothing wildly exciting about a prayer-meeting. Yet, like the seaside lodgings and the Palace Beautiful, the Church has her own peculiar and compensating charms. She quickly dispels all unhappy illusions caused by superficial impressions. To those who enter her portals she offers coigns of vantage from which they may inhale the delicious fragrance of the fairest flowers and enjoy a prospect that ravishes the vision and captivates the heart.

And, after all, it is just that view for which we are all hungry. I have amused myself, since taking Mark Rutherford down from my shelf for the purposes of this article, by turning over the pages hastily, and noticing his constant references to starlit walks. Now he is worried, and that sight of the stars—that sense of the infinite—'extinguishes all mean cares.' On another occasion he is oppressed by the conviction that 'there is nothing in him.' He walks beneath the stars and feels that, in a universe of such incomprehensible immensity, there is room for every worm that crawls, and, therefore, a place for him. Again, he is aflame with anger. He walks beneath the stars, and, 'reflecting on the great idea of God, and on all that it involves, his animosities are softened and his heat against his brother is cooled.' We have found at least a dozen such passages in this one book. They are suggestive. Mark Rutherford surely means that the infinite cures everything. He means that, to conquer our besetments, to subdue our passions, to realize our best selves, we need the window open toward Jerusalem, the sunny outlook on the eternal. And he means, too, that to obtain that vision splendid we dare not despise the most uninviting ministries. 'A dismal row of plain-looking houses'—*so they seemed.* 'What we thought were the fronts were the backs, and the fronts faced the bay. They had pretty gardens on the other side, and a glorious sunny prospect over the ocean'—*so they actually were.*

Somebody has said that God must be very fond of commonplace folk—He makes so many of them. Life is full of dingy-looking places and shabby-looking people. But we shall do well to think the thing all over again before, on that ground, we exclude them from our affections and our confidence. As the years come and go we learn that the best and most satisfying springs are those from which, on their discovery, we expected least. Our most treasured friends are not always those with whom we fell in love at first sight. In his wonderful *Life of the Bee* Maeterlinck tells us at least one thing to which we may do well to take heed. At one time, he says, it was almost impossible to introduce into a hive an alien queen. The myriad toilers would at once assume that she was an enemy, and set about her destruction. But now the apiarist introduces the new queen in an iron cage, with a door skilfully constructed of wax and honey. The bees immediately commence to gnaw their way through the door to murder the intruder; but, in the tedious process, they are compelled carefully to observe the royal prisoner. And, by the time that the waxen palisade is demolished, they have learned to love her; and they finish up by doing her homage and becoming her devoted slaves. So true is it that the forbidding may eventually become the fascinating; the repulsive may end in the romantic; the prose may kindle into poetry; the sombre shadows may dissolve into radiant reality; the dingy lodgings may open to us dazzling horizons; life's mocking mirages often pass into most satisfying streams.

If it comes to attractive exteriors and enticing advertisements, theology cannot hold a candle to theatricals, nor prayer-meetings to picture-shows. But they have most radiant outlooks for all that. And have we not somewhere read of One who is spoken of by those who are happy enough to know Him as the fairest among ten thousand and the altogether lovely? Yet, when first they saw Him, He was to them as a root out of a dry ground, having no beauty that they should desire Him! But I have said enough by this time to show that the experiences of Mark Rutherford and Mary Mardon have warnings of the gravest moment for us all.

VI

THE CLIFFS OF DOVER

MRS. BARCLAY, in *The Rosary*, says a fine thing about those towering walls of chalk that guard the English coast. She describes her heroine—the Hon. Jane Champion—returning to England after an absence of two years. 'The white cliffs of Dover,' she says, 'gradually became more solid and distinct, until at length they rose from the sea, a strong white wall, emblem of the undeniable purity of England, the stainless honour and integrity of her throne, her Church, her Parliament, her courts of justice, and her dealings at home and abroad, whether with friend or foe. *Strength and Whiteness!* thought Jane, as she paced the steamer's deck; and, after a two years' absence, her heart went out to her native land.'

'Strength and Whiteness'—those two are inseparable.

The principle holds, of course, in the realm to which Mrs. Barclay specially applies it. Nobody who has once read Macaulay's essay on Lord Clive can ever forget the classic and stately sentences in which the historian pays his tribute to British rule in India. He shows that the stability of our government lies in its justice, its uprightness, its trustworthiness. 'English valour and English intelligence,' he says, 'have done less to extend and to preserve our oriental empire than English veracity. All that we could have gained by imitating the doublings, the evasions, the fictions, the perjuries, which have been employed against us is as nothing when compared with what we have gained by being the one Power in India on whose word reliance can be placed. No oath which superstition can devise, no hostage, however precious, inspires a hundredth part of the confidence which is produced by the "Yea, yea" and "Nay, nay" of a British envoy. The greatest advantage which a Government can possess is to be the one trustworthy Government in the midst of Governments which nobody can trust. This advantage we enjoy in Asia.' It would be difficult to subpœna a witness more impressive or convincing.

But there is one most pertinent application of the principle for which, it seems to me, the times are clamorously and insistently calling. In these lands, and in these days, two truths demand iteration and emphasis in relation to all matters of politics and all affairs of State. Let it be said, as plainly as language can assert it, first of all that the nation needs strong men, and then that the *strong* men are the *white* men. That people has fallen on very evil days that finds itself in the grip, and at the mercy, of the professional politician. A pair of instances, both very much to the point, will enforce my meaning. The first is from Sir James Stephen's *Essays in Ecclesiastical Biography.* The professor points out that William Wilberforce lived his parliamentary life as a contemporary of William Pitt, Edmund Burke, Charles James Fox, and Richard Brinsley Sheridan. Here was a galaxy of brilliance —the most polished and powerful orators who ever awoke the classic echoes of St. Stephen's! Wilberforce's figure conveyed the inevitable impression of insignificance. Yet when he rose to address the Commons the House instantly crowded. Members held their breaths to listen. The little reformer spoke with an authority rarely wielded by the greatest masters. He was heard in a silence, and with a respect, which were never accorded to those illustrious statesmen whose utterances are to this day read in schools and colleges as models of rhetoric. And why? There is only one reason for it. Like Sir Galahad—

> His strength was as the strength of ten,
> Because his heart was pure.

The second of these companion pictures is from
Sir Henry W. Lucy's *Sixty Years in the Wilder-
ness*. In the last chapter of this fascinating book
the author draws a striking contrast between John
Bright and Benjamin Disraeli. 'Disraeli,' he says,
'lacked two qualities, failing which true eloquence
is impossible: he was never quite in earnest, and he
was not troubled by dominating conviction.' Now
for the contrast. 'John Bright, perhaps the finest
orator known to the House of Commons in the last
half of the nineteenth century, was morally and
politically the antithesis of Disraeli. To a public
man this atmosphere of acknowledged sincerity and
honest conviction is a mighty adjunct of power.'
Here, then, in both pictures, we have the conjunc-
tion of whiteness and strength; incorruptibility
wedded to omnipotence. This marriage was made
in heaven. These two God hath joined together.

I have emphasized the national and political
aspect of the truth because the conviction grows
upon me that we sadly need the reminder. But
I should be exceedingly sorry to leave the impres-
sion that the application was by any means exclu-
sive. It is just as true of every walk of life and of
every department of service. I turn the lantern on
my own heart and study and pulpit, and upon those
of my brethren. In a recently published work, the

Rev. J. D. Jones, of Bournemouth, says a very
gracious thing concerning a ministerial friend of
his: 'In print his sermons are almost dull, as they
are certainly lacking in literary style.   But when
you come into his presence, the transparent honesty
and obvious saintliness of the man lend to his words
compelling and subduing force.'   'I cannot under-
stand your minister's power,' said a visitor to a
friend of mine who was a member of a Midland
church to which a man ministered who was not a
great preacher, perhaps, but who was a great saint;
'I cannot understand your minister's power,' he
said; 'I do not see very much in him.'   'Ah,' re-
plied the host, 'you see, there are thirty years of
holy life behind every sermon.'   There is no doubt
about it.   Whiteness is strength.   The white men
wield the sceptre, and we are all their slaves.

But the last word has yet to be said.   A most
interesting play of language occurs in the last book
of the Bible: 'I saw a strong angel proclaiming
with a loud voice, Who is *worthy* to open the book
and to loose the seals thereof?   And no man in
heaven, nor in earth, neither under the earth, was
able to open the book, neither to look thereon.'   It
will be noticed that the words *worthy* and *able* are
treated as though they were interchangeable and
synonymous, as indeed they are.   The *worthy* are

the *able*. Whiteness is strength. Might is not always right, but right is always. might. God is not always on the side of the big battalions, but the big battalions are always on the side of God. That is why the meek inherit the earth. 'And I beheld, and lo, a *Lamb*—sublimest symbol of innocence, whiteness, meekness—and He came and took the book. And they sang a new song, saying, Thou art worthy! . . . Worthy is the Lamb!' And just because He was worthy, it followed, as the night the day, that He was able.

We have traced this truth from the cliffs of Dover right up to the dizziest pinnacle to which human eyes can peer. From the great white stone to the Great White Throne this thing holds grandly true. Whiteness and strength; innocence and omnipotence; right and might,—they go side by side, and hand in hand, both in the heavens above and on the earth beneath. That was what Mrs. Barclay's heroine saw in symbol as she gazed upon the white walls of old England. And the seer who, from the isle that is called Patmos, beheld the gleaming towers and shining turrets of the Celestial City, saw nothing greater.

VII

THE ORGANIST

THE organist is an ecclesiastical vagabond. He is a nomad and a nondescript. He lives in a kind of No-man's land. In the rationale of our spiritual economy he has never been provided with a home. We have never taken the trouble to place him. We have ministers, and we know why we have them. Deacons and teachers and choirs we have, and their contribution to our worship is well defined and clearly understood. But we allow the organist, as organist, to hover spectrally on the frontiers of our religious domain. We have never made up our minds as to whether he is simply a cog-wheel in the cold mechanism of our church organization or one of the controlling forces of the inner life of the sanctuary. Is he, in a word, one of those reviving, quickening, spiritual factors that are an essential part of our worship and testimony, or is he merely a necessary appendage, a convenient adjunct, an entertaining auxiliary? Is he a member of the family, or merely a distant relative, or, perchance, a nodding acquaintance? We offer him a chair—

or at any rate a stool—on Sundays and at choir practices; then he folds his tent, like the Arab, and silently steals away. We scarcely know where to place him. Is he inside or outside? Is he a partner or a passenger? In fairness to him, and in justice to ourselves, we ought to face the problem. We must classify and locate him. Too long the Church has said to the organist, 'The *minister* we know, and the *choir* we know, but who are *you*!'

Now, there are very few subjects that have betrayed their exponents into more obvious confusion of thought than the attempt to define the exact relationship existing between minstrelsy and ministry. The case for the organist has never yet been satisfactorily stated, either from the purely musical or from the purely ecclesiastical view-point. Here, for example, Charles Santley, in his *Reminiscences,* tells us that his master, Nava, at the Conservatoire at Milan, used to insist 'that the object of music was to give greater expression and emphasis to the words.' Which, of course, is unadulterated nonsense. It is true enough of certain forms of vocal music, but the sweeping and merciless dictum ruthlessly excommunicates the blackbird and the thrush, the nightingale and the canary, and at the same time cuts the throat of our unhappy organist. If we subscribe to the daring proposition we condemn the

'Dead March' and the 'Wedding March' as inanities, and all our organist's wordless voluntaries become impertinences of the worst kind. It is clear, therefore, that, whilst our Milanese master is indisputably right in insisting on the clear enunciation of every syllable, when there are syllables to enunciate, he has not spoken the whole truth. He has failed to supply us with a practical theory that will include both the goldfinch and the organist, the two great wordless minstrels in the temples of Nature and Grace.

Now, if our theologians had read their Bibles as carefully as our organists have read their music, they would most certainly have discovered that the Scriptures have some very fine things to say about the organist. Here, for instance, is quite a cluster of great Old Testament stories which should have helped us to solve our problem long ago. Look at this one: Jehoram, the wicked King of Israel, and Jehoshaphat, the good King of Judea, have for a while joined forces that they might fight side by side against the Moabites. But in the course of the campaign their united armies fall into sore straits, and Jehoshaphat longs to hear some guiding voice. In his perplexity he hungers for fellowship with the skies. His soul ached to speak with God. 'Is there not a prophet?' he inquired. Elisha is found, and three kings stand before him, and beg him to prophesy. But the lips of the seers are sealed; he has no message; he is dumb. Then he cried: 'Bring me a minstrel! And it came to pass, when the minstrel played, that the hand of the Lord came upon Elisha, and he prophesied'! Now, here is a clear-cut case in which the organist was simply indispensable to the minister. The prophet could not prophesy without the minstrel. The player was the preacher's inspiration—a minister to the minister. The music of the minstrel directly contributed to a magnificent spiritual result. 'When the minstrel played, the hand of the Lord came upon Elisha, and he prophesied.'

Two other instances of a similar kind will leap to the memory of every reader: (1) When Saul heard the music of the psaltery and the tabret and the pipe and the harp, the Spirit of the Lord came upon him, and he prophesied, and was turned into another man; (2) When David took his harp and played before Saul 'the evil spirit departed from him.' The point is that in each case we recognize the organist. It is instrumental music, pure and simple. There is no question of words, whether clearly or indistinctly enunciated. And in each case the language admits of no second interpretation; an emphatically spiritual effect was produced. We must be honest, even though we be theologians; we must be fair, even towards an organist. None of the facts must be blinked.

Now, we venture to think that a working hypothesis can be built upon these facts. Two irresistible conclusions emerge. The first is that the organist is clearly part and parcel of our spiritual economy. Indeed, these three graceful old stories, if they mean anything, seem to show that we need our friend the organist in every department of our religious enterprise. For, in the first two cases, it was through his agency that the Divine Spirit was received; and in the third case it was by means of his melodious ministry that the evil spirit was expelled. These are the two great essential functions of the Church in every age—to invoke a fresh inrush of spiritual enlightenment and reviving fervour, and to exorcise and expel all that is unrighteous, unholy, and unclean. And if, as these stories plainly show, the organist can help the Church to fulfil these two magnificent missions and to realize this sublime spiritual ideal, then let all pastors and deacons and teachers and singers stand up and say, *God bless the organist!*

But, lest our friend of the music-stool should become exalted above measure by the brilliance, as of the seventh heaven, of this Old Testament revelation, we hasten to emphasize the second principle that clearly emerges from its beatific splendours. It is manifest that the music of the minstrel is not an end in itself. Just as the work of the minister is not in itself spiritually effective, but is the channel through which the excellency of the divine power may communicate itself, so the harmonies of the organ are but a *means* of grace. The language is wonderfully exact and explicit: 'When the minstrel played, *the hand of the Lord* came upon Elisha,' and it was the hand of the Lord that wrought the resultant miracle. We hazard the suggestion that if our pastors and officers and members would spend half an hour in the careful contemplation of these exquisite old records, their eyes would be so illumined that they would detect an aureole encircling the brows of the organist. And if our minstrels would pore over these fragrant pages for a while they would feel the thrill of a new ecstasy in their avocation, and glorify their talents with a fresh consecration. An added sweetness and dignity would lurk in those lovely notes that come trilling and shuddering down from the organ. And the gracious ministries of our minstrelsy would anticipate that home of the eternal harmonies in the heart and centre of whose melodies the Lord himself delightedly abides.

VIII

THE JACKASS AND THE KANGAROO

A MINISTERIAL friend of mine was recently travelling in the far east of Australia. On his return he penned a most picturesque account of the wilds and wonders of the Queensland bush. And, in the process of his cinematographic description of a glorious motor-ride, he includes this realistic and characteristic touch: 'In the heart of the bush,' he says, 'we came upon a tragedy that must often be enacted amongst the animal dwellers of the great solitude—a kangaroo, a mother, unable to resist the pangs and pains thrust upon her by her destiny, lay dead upon the roadside, and above, on a branch of a tree, stood a pair of laughing-jackasses, guffawing their loudest, as if life knew no tragedy and no pain.'

Here, then, is a painting, skilfully finished, before which we may profitably pause. And the charm of it—as of all great pictures—is that it is so true to life. The laughing-jackass and the dead kangaroo! I always keep up one of my sleeves a microscopic—a very microscopic—naturalist, and an equally microscopic philosopher up the other. I unrolled my friend's picture to my naturalist. 'Ah, yes,' he said, 'there you have the jackass all over; that's the way of the bird!' I turned to my other sleeve, and showed the picture to the philosopher. 'Ah, yes,' he said, 'there you have life in miniature; that's the way of the world!'

'The way of the bird' and 'the way of the world.' What do these gentlemen mean? Let us probe a little. Now, the jackass has a literature of his own. I suppose the most captivating and convincing description of our bush comedian that has ever been penned is the classical sketch by Frank Buckland. That most genial and most winsome of all British naturalists simply revelled in his study of the jackass. And he was particularly amused by the very trait that arrested my friend on his tour. He pillories him thus: 'The bird has a custom of laughing in a most exasperating fashion,' he says, 'when a misfortune happens to travellers. Thus, when a wagon loaded with goods breaks down in some desolate region on a long march, and the owner is at his wits' end to get it right again, a laughing-jackass is sure to appear at the top of a neighbouring tree and laugh in the most aggravating manner at the miserable condition of the traveller, till the woods

resound with his merry "Ha, ha, ha! He, he, he!
Ho, ho, ho!"' This is very interesting. We are
grateful to Mr. Buckland and to my friend for
drawing our attention to so curious a phenomenon.
But this chapter is not to be understood as a fugitive
excursion into natural history. I am attracted to
the theme by quite other considerations. For it is
surely as clear as noonday that the incident is true
to life in the deepest sense. We are for ever and
ever discovering, with a shock of surprise, that the
laughing-jackass is never far away from the dead
kangaroo. At every turn of our pilgrimage we see
comedy stand grinning cheek by jowl with tragedy.
The world is made up of the most discordant and
incongruous juxtapositions.

Among the treasures in the Sydney Art Gallery
is Sir Luke Fildes' famous painting entitled 'The
Widower.' On the right-hand side of the picture
sits the poor toiler, with his sick child on his knee.
One overwhelming bereavement has already over-
taken him, and another stares him in the face. His
brow is clouded with uttermost sorrow and per-
plexity. He looks at his child and seems to say, 'If
only *she* were here!' And on the left-hand side of
the picture are the younger children playing on the
floor, laughing and crowing in their merriment.
They are not old enough to understand; but their

delight seems cruelly to mock his despair. Have we not here the story of the laughing-jackass and the dead kangaroo over again? The thing occurs hourly. As the mourners return broken-hearted from the graveside they are tortured by the mad melody of wedding-bells from a neighbouring belfry. Edward FitzGerald somewhere says that there are no lines in our literature so pathetically expressive of the soul's deepest emotions as the familiar song of Robert Burns:

> Ye banks and braes o' bonnie Doon,
>   How can ye bloom so fresh and fair?
> Ye little birds, how can ye sing,
>   And I so weary, full of care?

Who is there that, passing through some deep valley of weeping, has not been stabbed to the quick by the laughter on the hills? I shall never forget the day on which I left the Homeland. I was about to set sail for lands in which I should be the veriest stranger. I passed, on my way to the ship, through the crowded London streets, every one of which was endeared to me by old associations and enriched by fond memories. I was accompanied by those who were all the world to me, those who, like myself, were calling up all the reserve powers of the will to nerve them for the wrench of parting. And I remember how I was mocked by the sounds of the city streets. My soul was in tears; but who cared? People were chattering; crowds were jostling; news-boys were shouting; all London was sunlit and gay. It seemed as though the old haunts were glad to see me go. The laughter tore and lacerated my spirit. The jackass seems a hideous incongruity in the presence of the dead kangaroo.

The parable has an obvious application to public affairs. There are enough dead kangaroos lying about the world, in all conscience! Our tragedies are tremendous. At the moment of writing Italy and Turkey are at war. France and Germany are scowling angrily at each other across their frontiers. China is convulsed in the throes of a huge revolution. Spain and Portugal are in a state of seething tumult and disorder. At our own doors the social conditions are full of disquiet and unrest. Strikes and lock-outs are the order of the day. We are not alarmists; we see in all this no cause for panic. The pessimist is completely out of court. But, on the other hand, we do submit that these things call for a certain public seriousness and gravity. The newspapers should cause every decent citizen furi-ously to think. Yet we see small evidence of seri-ous thought; quite otherwise. The pursuit of pleas-ure—and not always of the noblest pleasure—was never so deliriously feverish. The woods seem to resound with the untimely giggle of the laughing-jackass; and, with so many tragedies about us, the notes grate harshly on our ears. We venture a pertinent application. If things have become so serious that Australia needs to build battleships and compel all her sons to bear arms, then things have become far too serious for pugilistic orgies and similar carnivals of inanity. There is no doubt about it. The laughing-jackass is quite out of place beside the dead kangaroo.

We pause reverently for a moment before daring to suggest a still deeper consideration in closing. Perhaps, perhaps this is why our Gospels present to us the sad and stricken face of a Man of Sorrows. The smitten soul, turning aside like a wounded deer from the herd, simply could not endure a gay or mirthful Saviour. I know a lady who dismissed her doctor because she could not bear the levities with which he thought to brighten her. Her nerves winced and squirmed beneath his jokes and chatter. It is a curious fact that there are more suicides in summer than in winter, and more in genial and sunny climes than in sterner temperatures. The reason is obvious. The brightness and gaiety of the world mock the bruised and battered spirit and drive it to despair. A tearless Saviour would have re-pelled the very souls that Jesus came to save; but One over whose crushed spirit all the waves of grief have surged must be the natural refuge of all penitent and contrite hearts so long as time shall last. It is this harmony of the emotions, this subtle and unfathomable wealth of infinite sympathy, that has led millions to sing with choked and trembling voices:

> Rock of Ages, cleft for me,
> Let me hide myself in Thee;
> Let the water and the blood,
> From Thy riven side which flowed,
> Be of sin the double cure,
> Save me from its guilt and power.

There is a world of tender significance in the incongruous tragedy which the motor-car passed by the side of the track.

IX

OUR RUBBISH-HEAPS

THE great bush solitudes had taken the place of the bustling streets. He—an Australian minister on holiday—rested on a fallen tree beside the dusty track. He raised his hat to the loveliness and bathed his brow in the loneliness that pervaded everything. It was with him as when a great steamer stops in mid-ocean to allow her engines to cool. The thud of the propeller, the vibration of the machinery, are felt no longer; the stillness is uncanny. He drew from his breast-pocket his Bible, and, his mind recurring to his own attempts to build the city of God among the haunts of men, he turned to the stately old story of Nehemiah. He read on, undisturbed by the drowsy hum of insects and the merrier songs of birds, until arrested by Sanballat's question: 'What do these feeble Jews? Will they *revive* the stones out of the heaps of the *rubbish* which are burned?' It was an awakening phrase— *a revival from a rubbish-heap!* He laid the open

147

Bible on the mossy log beside him and lost himself
in contemplation.

And, even as he pondered, a new object presented
itself to his hungry mind. From the depths of the
bush on the distant hill-side great wreathing
columns of smoke curled skywards, occasionally
shot through by fierce flashes of flame. Straining
his ears to listen, he caught the crash of falling
trees, and thought he could detect the crackle and
roar of the fires as the monsters yielded themselves
to the devouring element. Straining his eyes to see,
he dimly discerned the figures of men moving here
and there, superintending the work of demolition
and destruction. They were clearing away the
maple and the myrtle, the wattle and the gum, to
make room for the apple and the apricot, the peach-
tree and the pear. And the preacher, as he watched,
caught himself echoing Sanballat's question: 'Will
they bring a revival out of a rubbish-heap? Will
they obtain riches from refuse?' These were com-
panion pictures—this picture in the Bible and this
picture in the bush; and, as he gazed upon them
side by side, several clear-cut thoughts emerged.
He saw that rubbish-heaps fill a large place in the
domestic economy of a world like this. And he
saw that an element of such enormous magnitude
must be governed by laws. Refuse must have its

fixed rules. The slag-heap must have its statutes. They have!

There is the law of *deterioration.* From the picture in the Bible and the picture in the bush it becomes clear that all material things, though as sacred as the Temple or as natural as the forest flowers, are on their way to the rubbish-heap. It sounds like a death-knell to the materialist. Materialism, unmasked, appears as the religion of the rubbish-heap. It is heavy tidings, too, for the ritualist; for Ritualism stands in perilous relationship to the rubbish-heap. 'Now abideth'—what? Altars? vestments? crosses? creeds? catechisms? confessions? 'Now abideth faith, hope, love—these three; and the greatest of these is love.' The moth is in our fairest fabrics, and our holiest temples totter to their fall. 'And as some spake of the Temple, how it was adorned with goodly stones and gifts, Jesus said: As for these things which ye behold, the days will come in the which there shall not be left one stone upon another that shall not be cast down.' That is significant. It is well to set our affections on the things for which the rubbish-heap can have no terrors.

There is the law of *occupation.* For Nehemiah, in the one picture, and the settler in the other, find the ground not fallow, but occupied. Moss and lichen cover every stone. Giant trees, twining creepers, shapely ferns, and waving grasses fight for every inch of soil. Rank weeds and spear-like leaves peer out from all the interstices. Every crack and cranny, every corner and crevice, is occupied. Nature abhors a vacuum. Wherever the foot of man has failed to tread, wherever the hand of man has failed to labour, God's innumerable and invisible agriculturists plough and harrow, sow and reap, and produce the bewildering beauties of the bush. Hannibal's military precept of preoccupation dominates the rubbish-heap. The moss and the lichen are on the stones of Jerusalem because no Nehemiah has come to build the city. The wattle and the gum abound on the hill-side simply because no man has planted apricots or pears. Is it not ever so? The mind becomes a wilderness of foul imaginations because clean and wholesome thoughts have not been planted there. The heart becomes, like Jerusalem, a wilderness and a desolation because the kingdom of Christ has never been established there. Evil evolves where good evacuates.

There is the law of *elevation*. The question is: What makes rubbish rubbish? The term is obviously not absolute, but relative. A lady's hat is a milliner's dream to-day. To-morrow—a new style having come in—it is its mistress's despair. What has so suddenly changed delight to disgust, and made the fashion of yesterday the folly of to-day? It is the new style. And it is always the new style, whether of dresses or of dreadnoughts, that flings the satisfaction of one day to the slag-heap of the next. What has made the maple and the laurel look like rubbish to the settler? The parrots and the kangaroos see no change to account for his vandalism. The aboriginals did not find it necessary to hack down trees and fire the undergrowth. Why, then, this fury of axe and torch and gunpowder? It is the conception of an orchard that has done it. That is the 'new style.' A man dreams of apples, and he burns the virgin bush. Then, in his orchard he sees the glint of gold! The soil is auriferous! The fruit-trees become firewood that he may seize the precious metal. Later on, in peril of a watery grave, he flings his very gold into the ocean that he may save his life. Bush, fruit, gold, each in their turn become rubbish, flung to the slag-heap by the alluring force of a higher attraction. Nor is life itself the last stage. The martyrs cheerfully threw even life away, fascinated by still greater wealth. Had not Paul his rubbish-heap? He counted all things but loss for the excellency of the knowledge of Christ Jesus his Lord, for whom he had suffered the loss of all things, and did count them but dung, that he might win Christ. The rubbish-heap can have no grander word written of it than that.

There is the law of *transformation*. God makes His loveliest roses out of rubbish. The charred ashes of yesterday's bush nourish the roots of to-morrow's orchard. If the refuse of the ages had been allowed to accumulate, the world would be un-inhabitable. The air would be heavy with pesti-lence. We bury our rubbish, and it all comes back to us in fruits and flowers. Its resurrection body is divine.

It is just here that the Church finds her most acute problem. In every community there are crowds of people who have gone to the wall. They feel crushed and beaten. Under our fierce competitive system the iron law of the survival of the fittest has flung them on the social slag-heap, and they know it. They hate the churches, because the churches are old, and they think that if the churches had done their duty, things would not be as they are. They forget that, if the churches had *not* done their duty, things would be ten thousand times worse than they are. They snatch at every social quackery and political panacea. Now, the Church's mission is to do for this ruined mass what Nehemiah did for the rubbish-heaps of Jerusalem—to build out of them the city of God. 'Will they bring a revival out of a rubbish-heap?' asks Sanballat. Of course. A rubbish-heap is God's raw material. A revival is His finished product. Let the Church get to work. She alone is equipped for so divine a duty. If she fail, her collapse will be the disaster of the ages. In that melancholy event, this social rubbish-heap will become, like all untransformed rubbish-heaps, the menace of mankind and the peril of the world. In it all pestilential fever-germs will breed and multiply. Anarchisms and revolutions will fill the air with shrieks and screams. But the Church of Jesus Christ knows how to transform this mass of refuse into a field of roses. Paul understood the magic secret. He looked upon the unbridled lust, the grinding tyranny, and the hideous idolatry of the city of the Caesars, and was unabashed. And he gave his reason. The gospel, he said, is the power of God unto transformation. He saw that the foulest filth of Rome might become the fairest fragrance of the New Jerusalem.

X

LIFE'S INVISIBLE CONSTABULARY

'I'm always a-moving on, sir,' cried poor Jo, wiping away his grimy tears with his arm. 'I've always been a-moving on and a-moving on ever since I was born. *Where* can I possibly move to, sir, more nor I do move?'

'My instructions don't go to that,' said the constable. 'My instructions are that you are to move on. I've told you so five hundred times.'

'Well, but really, constable, you know,' observed Mr. Snagsby (to whom poor Jo's appeal had been addressed), 'really that does seem a question. *Where*, you know?'

So far Charles Dickens and *Bleak House*. Mr. Snagsby and poor Jo were indisputably right. It is the easiest thing in the world to keep moving on. 'But *where*, you know?' For it is the hardest thing in the world so to direct our movements that each change shall represent a real advance, and constitute itself a distinct contribution towards the attainment of an ultimate goal. By a sure instinct we ask each

other on the street, not 'Are you getting on?' be-
cause that matters little, but '*How* are you getting
on?' because that matters everything. 'Really,' as
Mr. Snagsby said, 'that does seem a question—
where, you know?'

Now, movement is the law of life. The police-
man told J$_0$ that he must move or be locked up.
But the greater constabulary of the solar system
are very much more severe. They tell us that we
must move or be put to death.

Drummond's savage is a case in point. Says the
amiable Professor: 'When we meet him first he is
sitting, we shall suppose, in the sun. Let us also
suppose—and it requires no imagination to suppose
it—that he has no wish to do anything else than
sit in the sun, and that he is perfectly contented and
perfectly happy. Nature around him, visible and
invisible, is as still as he is, as inert apparently, as
unconcerned. Neither molests the other; they have
no connexion with each other. Yet it is not so.
That savage is the victim of a conspiracy. Nature
has designs upon him. She wants to move him.
How does she set about moving him? By moving
herself.' The sun goes down; he must move on or
freeze. The time rolls on; he must move or starve.
The roar of the wild beast is heard; he must move
or be eaten. *He moves!*

It could easily be shown that these invisible constables have other and even surer methods of moving us on. They give us work to do, and wreck it for us so soon as we have done it, in order to make us do it all again. We build a house. Before the workmen have removed the scaffolding millions upon millions of invisible hands have set to work to reduce the building to ruins. It is only a question of time, and they will have left it, like Solomon's Temple, with not one stone upon another. They are terribly afraid—those unseen constables— that we shall loiter and stand still. They tear our work to pieces, and demolish the very homes in which we live, for the sheer sake of compelling us to renew our toils. They overthrow Nineveh and Tyre and Athens and Jerusalem and Rome that we may build London and Paris and Buenos Ayres and Chicago and Melbourne. And they are tearing down these that we may build the New Jerusalem. They are always moving us on. We plough a field. We must harrow and sow it at once, or they will trample it down with their microscopic feet until it needs reploughing. We gaze upon our golden crop. We must reap it immediately or they will drench and destroy it before our very eyes. We garner our harvest. We must plough the field again, or they will sow such a crop of thorns and of thistles

as will make our backs ache even to look upon them.
No street-corner constable was ever so imperative,
so merciless, so tyrannical as are these. 'My in-
structions,' said the policeman to poor Jo, 'are that
you are to move on. I have told you so five hun-
dred times.' That is nothing. These other con-
stables have told us so five million times. They say
it from morning till night. They say it from baby-
hood to old age. They said it when the first day
dawned, and they will be saying it when the last
sun sets. It is 'Move on!' for ever and ever and
ever. And, to be doubly certain that we do move,
they move us! Whether we like it or not, whether
we sleep or wake, they hurl us through space at the
dizzy rate of thousands of miles an hour to greet the
sunrise; and in another direction they push us along
at the terrific speed of sixty thousand miles an hour
towards the summer-time. We are whirling and
spinning and rushing and flying from midnight till
noonday and noonday till midnight. These fearful
forces appal us with their everlasting cry of 'Move
on!' Poor Jo's sad plight was a mere circumstance
when compared with our own. And there is no
Mr. Snagsby to intercede with our constables!

The science of life hinges upon turning mere
movement into progress. Huxley once found him-
self being driven in a hansom cab at a breakneck

speed round and round a certain network of London streets. He had told the hackman to 'drive fast,' but had not instructed him as to his destination! It does not by any means follow that movement, even the most rapid movement, is necessarily progress. In the *Origin of Species* Darwin has a good deal to say about 'certain larvae that actually stand higher in the scale of organization than the mature animal into which they are afterwards developed.' Have we not witnessed the same phenomenon? There is, for example, all the difference imaginable between the *Mayflower*, as she crossed the Atlantic nearly three centuries ago, and the *Mauretania*, the pride of yesterday. The *Mayflower* was the 'larva,' the *Mauretania* the 'mature animal.' But the *Mayflower* was a house of prayer, a temple of worship, and, on every Atlantic breeze that blew, songs of praise were wafted to the skies. Concerning the maiden voyage of the palatial *Mauretania* a London paper says that the trip was rendered hideous by the brutal ferocity of gamblers and the horrid debauchery of drunkards. 'The smoking-room became a veritable Bedlam.' Match-stands, spittoons, glasses, soda-water bottles, trays, and chairs were flying in all directions. On arrival at New York the vessel was met by detectives, who had been warned by Marconigrams from the ship (a device of which the *Mayflower* could not boast and for which she had no such use). These officials straightway conducted the passengers to the Jefferson police-court. From the *Mayflower* to the *Mauretania* is a big 'move on'; but, in view of these records, one may be permitted to speculate as to how far the movement has represented a real advance. It sometimes happens, as Darwin says, that the larvae outstrip the mature animal.

The principle is capable of somewhat incisive individual applications. Ignorance, in the immortal allegory, moved on just as far as did Christian and Hopeful; but at the gates of the Celestial City 'the Shining Ones took him and carried him through the air to the door that I saw in the side of the hill and put him in there.' Movement kept pace with the movement of the pilgrims, but Progress made no advance at all. And perhaps the most appealing of all illustrations of this principle is Tom Hood's:

> I remember, I remember,
>   The fir-trees dark and high;
> I used to think their slender tops
>   Were close against the sky;
> It was a childish ignorance,
>   But now 'tis little joy
> To know I'm farther off from heaven
>   Than when I was a boy.

The larvae, that is to say, were in advance of the

mature animal which developed from them. The
unseen constabulary of the universe can move us
on; but it is not in their power to see that the move-
ment shall be progress. They move us on as the
wind moves the ships: it is for us to trim our sails
to suit our destinies. For there are two great prin-
ciples involved in getting on. There is the principle
of the *propeller,* and there is the principle of the
rudder. The propeller may make the pace, but only
so far as it is checked and directed and controlled
by the rudder can we be sure of 'getting there.' It
is so fatally easy to move on.

'But *where*?' cries poor Jo.

'Well, really, constable, you know,' says Mr.
Snagsby wistfully, 'really, constable, that does seem
a question. *Where,* you know?'

Mr. Snagsby is quite right. It is a question in-
deed!

XI

'SO MANY BEDS IN THE WARD!'

THAT was little Emmie's trouble: *So many beds in the ward!* The lines are almost too familiar to need quoting:

'Yes, and I will,' said Emmie, 'but then, if I call to the
  Lord,
How should He know that it's me? such a lot of beds in
  the ward!'
That was a puzzle for Annie. Again she considered and
  said:
'Emmie, you put out your arms, and you leave 'em outside
  on the bed—
The Lord has so much to see to! but, Emmie, you tell it
  Him plain,
It's the little girl with her arms lying out on the counter-
  pane.'

Now here, with an art that is all the more wonderful because it is the art that conceals art, Tennyson has stated for us one of the most acute problems of the Christian faith. *The Lord has so much to see to! Such a lot of beds in the ward!* These are the ugly thoughts that have come knocking at all our doors at some time or other. Did I say, 'at some time or other'? I mean at one especial time. These are the ugly thoughts that have entered all our heads just when the time came to pray. We were burdened. We hungered for a sense of the divine sympathy, the divine interest, the divine care. And, as we kneeled, little Emmie's question came dinning itself into our shuddering souls: 'The Lord has so much to see to! Such a lot of beds in the ward!' We rose disillusioned. When we kneeled, the place seemed like a shrine. When we rose, it was only a cupboard. When we kneeled, it seemed as though we were about to hold communion with the very skies. When we rose, the ceiling itself seemed to be grinning at our defeat. It was as though all the lamps of faith had been blown out. It was as though life's dearest companion had wilfully turned his back upon us. It was as though the doors of home had been suddenly slammed in our faces. 'The Lord has so much to see to! Such a lot of beds in the ward!'

These reflections have been suggested by a letter which has just reached me. It is from a gentleman who has gained, with marked distinction, two of the highest degrees obtainable on this side of the world. I mention this to show that the problem is not confined to poor little waifs in London hospitals. Here, on the one hand, we have little Emmie; and here, on the other, we have our brilliant university graduate. But in both cases the trouble is the same. 'I have given up praying!' my friend tells me. 'It seems so utterly incredible to me that a God who controls all worlds and inhabits all time can have patience to hear me speak to Him about my examinations, and my love-affairs, and my prospects.' Here then, quite clearly, we are face to face with little Emmie's puzzle over again. 'The Lord has so much to see to! Such a lot of beds in the ward!' Little Emmie stated the case from the standpoint of the child; the letter states it from the standpoint of the scholar. That is all.

Let me turn for a moment to current literature. Here on my desk is a London magazine containing an article by Miss Marie Corelli. It is not written in that lady's best vein. I am not sure that it is quite worthy of her. Her whole argument seems to be that the Lord has far too much to see to—that there are too many beds in the wards—to permit of His taking an individual interest either in a child in a London hospital or in a university graduate in Australia. She refers to the Most High as 'that tremendous Omnipotence to whose intelligent action we owe our very being—the Generator of universes

—the Creator of everything the eyes can see, the ears can hear, or the brain can imagine.' And she scorns the very idea that 'we, the children of one out of a million million vast productive epochs, should be found assuming a certain "swaggering" posture before this ever-present Divine.'

Here, then, we have the selfsame problem stated in three different ways: first, by a puny little patient in the children's hospital, then by a graduate of an Australian university, and once again by a modern novelist. And each one of us, if we cared and dared, could state it afresh in the throbbing terms of some profound personal experience. A book published some time ago told the story of 'old Mr. Westfield, a preacher of the Independent persuasion in a certain Yorkshire town, who was discoursing one Sunday with his utmost eloquence on the power of prayer. He suddenly stopped, passed his hands slowly over his head—a favourite gesture—and said, in dazed tones: "I do not know, my friends, whether you ever tried praying; for my part, I gave it up long ago as a bad job." The poor old gentleman never preached again. They spoke of the strange seizure that he had in the pulpit, and very cheerfully and kindly contributed to the pension which the authorities of the chapel allowed him. I knew him five-and-twenty years ago, a

gentle old man addicted to botany, who talked of
anything but spiritual experiences. I have often
wondered with what sudden flash of insight he
looked into his own soul that day, and saw himself
bowing down silent before an empty shrine.'

It is a great mystery, a very great mystery. And
yet—and yet—when you come to think of it, it is
all wonderfully and exquisitely simple. 'The Lord
has so much to see to!' It all turns on that. 'The
Lord has so much to see to!' *But what if He has?*
Is it not an almost universal experience that the
people who have most to see to are the very people
who see to each separate thing most thoroughly?
If a piece of work wants doing, we ask the busy
man to do it. He will consent without making a
fuss, and he will do the work well. 'So many beds
in the ward!' *And what if there are?* The mothers
who have most mouths to feed are the best mothers,
after all! We recall the recitation that was so popu-
lar some years ago. It told of a father and mother
struggling to support a large family. A handsome
offer came from a childless home. Would they, who
had so many, part with one? Father and mother
lit a candle and went from room to room among
their slumbering bairns; but they found each as
dear as though each were their only child. 'So
many beds!' said little Emmie. 'So many beds!'

said the tempter with his bags of gold. But when the many beds were visited the parents shook their heads over each. Not one could be spared. Indeed, the experience of this old world of ours shows conclusively that those children turn out best who come of large families. Darwin makes a great point of that. So that it is false to fact that a child gets more care if his is the only cot in the house. All experience goes to prove that a child is enriched, and not impoverished, when the parents have 'so much to see to'—'so many beds in the' home! It is fair, therefore, to say that there is not even a *prima facie* case to be made out for the fear which assailed the faith of our little sick waif, our Master of Arts, and our distinguished authoress. There is absolutely nothing in it. Reasoning, as alone we may, from things terrestrial to things celestial, it is clear that the great Father, who has so many children to see to, will take the very best care of each individual child, and will bring up His immense family with the greatest credit to Himself.

But even if, in spite of all this, the argument be allowed the honour of serious analysis, it is so easy to expose its fallacy! It will be noticed that the real difficulty, in each case, lies in the greatness of God. It seemed incredible to little Emmie, to our Master of Arts, and to Miss Corelli that a God who is 'the Generator of universes and the Creator of everything' can be concerned with the cares of the individual. Now the trouble is, not that they have made God to seem too great, but that they have not made Him great enough. They have belittled Him! Now, how great is God? That is the real question! Is He great to the point of absolute infinity? Is He, or is He not? Now, if God is great to the point of infinity, it follows, beyond all controversy, that there is no stick or stone in all His universes of which He is not perpetually cognizant and conscious. Or—to put it the other way—if there is a feather or a straw blowing about the solar system which has, for a fraction of a second, eluded His knowledge or escaped His observation, then, by just so much, His greatness falls short of infinity. If, therefore, I do really believe that God is not only great enough to be 'the Generator of universes and Creator of everything,' but great enough to be infinite, then I cannot help believing that no sparrow falls to the ground without His notice and that the very hairs of my head are all numbered. This has never been better stated than by Faber:

O Majesty unspeakable and dread!
  Wert Thou less mighty than Thou art,
Thou wert, O God, too great for our belief,
  Too little for our heart.

But greatness which is infinite makes room
  For all things in its lap to lie;
We should be crushed by a magnificence
  Short of infinity.

But what is infinite must be a home,
  A shelter for the meanest life,
Where it is free to make its greatest growth
  Far from the touch of strife.

Yes; there are many whose hearts have ached in sympathy with those of little Emmie, and our Master of Arts, and our eminent novelist. They have known the anguish of the empty shrine. Let them turn their faces in the direction I have tried to indicate. And if they will follow that road they will find that it leads home, and they will rest sweetly when they get there!

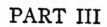
PART III

PART VII.

THE LAW OF THE LANE

Who that has lived in England has not stored, among his chiefest treasures, his memories of the old English country lane—its serpentine folds, its gentle undulations, its over-arching oaks, its delicious and fragrant hedgerows, its twitter of birds, its hum of insects, and its glimpses of golden buttercups in the spreading fields beyond? All these will haunt him till his last sun sets.

We have heard a great deal since then of the rule of the road; but the lane has a law of its own; and the law of the lane is an infinitely loftier and an infinitely lovelier thing than the rule of the road. And that is saying much, for Mr. G. K. Chesterton, our greatest literary acrobat (notwithstanding his insatiable fondness for standing on his head), says that the indescribable charm of Dickens may be best summed up in one satisfying phrase used by one of his own characters. ' "My friend," said Mr. Perker's clerk to Job Trotter, "you've got *the key of the street."'* And, says Mr. Chesterton, 'Dickens himself had, in the most sacred and serious sense of the term, the key of the street.'

Few of us understand the street. Even when we step into it we step into it doubtfully, as into a house or room of strangers. Few of us see through the shining riddle of the street, the strange folk that belong to the street only—the street-walker or the street-arab, the nomads, who, generation after generation, have kept their ancient secrets in the full blaze of the sun. Of the street at night many of us know even less. The street at night is a great house locked up. But Dickens had, if ever man had, the key of the street. His earth was the stones of the street; his stars were the lamps of the street; his hero was the man of the street. He could open the inmost door of his house—the door that leads into that secret passage which is lined with houses and roofed with stars.

Yes, the street is a wonderful place—a place of mystery and dread. But the lane is more wonderful still; for the street conceals, whilst the lane reveals. The street is a place of secrecy; the lane is a palace of song. Even if a man is born who, like Charles Dickens, possesses the key of the street, he can at best but tell us what man is. But he who reads the riddle of the lane knows what God is.

In the lane 'earth is cramm'd with heaven, and every common bush afire with God.'

> Little flower, but if I could understand
> What you are, root and all, and all in all,
> I should know what God and man is.

Charles Kingsley used to say that, whenever he strolled down an English lane, he felt as though everything about him, every leaf, and bud, and flower, were saying something to him, and he was pained and oppressed by the feeling of his own density.

Yes, compared with the lane, the street is a sordid place. It has its charms, but its charms are for sale. It barters its beauties for gold. It was from the street that Bunyan caught his conception of Vanity Fair. The lane displays its shining wares no less attractively, but offers them without money and without price. Who has ever found quite the same satisfaction in an afternoon's shopping as we found in the old lane long ago? The wild flowers that the lane offered us in the spring-time, when the long winter was past and gone; the tangle of hawthorn and dog-rose and convolvulus that we found there in the summer; the nuts and blackberries of autumn, and the redder berries with which we decked the home in winter,—the lane was never without its treasures. And they were always freely ours. There was no stint in the lane. Is it not Lowell who tells us that—

> Bubbles we buy with a whole soul's tasking;
> 'Tis heaven alone that is given away,
> 'Tis only God may be had for the asking?

And then, too, the lane was a winding place. When we were young we puzzled over its crazy progress, and stupidly wished that it were straight. Since then we have had to do with the realities of life; and we have learned, by tiresome experience of their monotony, that the last word in art is a graceful curve. We have driven, it may be, along the great prairie roads of the Western world—roads that, looking back, seemed to come in an unbending line from the Atlantic, and that, looking forward, seemed to run in one unbending line to the foot-hills of the Rocky Mountains. Or we have made our weary progress along the great undeviating tracks that intersect the vast Australian plains, and that seem to run without a swerve from world's-end to world's-end. We have journeyed along the street which is called Straight, and our hearts have longed the while for the tortuous but romantic folds of the dear old lane at home. And for our tardy prefer-ence there is a reason, psychological, and deeply based. The road across the prairies, the track across the plains, the street which is called Straight, are untrue to life and experience. They are artificial, unnatural, forced. Life is a lane; it abounds in surprises; it twists and doubles, and curves and folds. We cannot know what is just beyond. We quickly lose sight of our yesterdays. We are kindly compelled to take our to-morrows on trust. As Klingle says:

> God broke our years to hours and days,
>   That, hour by hour, and day by day,
>   Just going on a little way,
> We might be able all along to keep quite strong,
> Should all the weight of life
> Be laid across our shoulders, and the future rife
> With woe and struggle, meet us face to face
> At just one place,
>   We could not go;
>   Our feet would stop, and so
> God lays a little on us every day.

That is the law of the lane.

And the last song that the birds are singing in the old lane is perhaps the blithest of them all. It tells us that life does not lose its romance as the years wear away. It was not until we had left the lane for twenty years that we discovered its beauty. We find far more pleasure in the winding path now than we did when we perspired on sultry summer afternoons beneath the weight of our baskets of nuts or buckets of blackberries. We were choked with dust and tired to death, and were too close to catch the lane's loveliness in its right perspective. All of which is hugely significant.

We set out on this ramble in the excellent company of Mr. Chesterton. Let us return to him. 'Mrs. Nickleby,' he says, 'stands for a great truth which we must not forget: the truth that experience is not in real life a saddening thing at all. The people who have had misfortunes are generally the people who love to talk about them. Experience is really one of the gaieties of old age, one of its dissipations. Mere memory becomes a kind of debauch. Experience may be disheartening to those who are foolish enough to try to co-ordinate it and to draw deductions from it; but to those happy souls, like Mrs. Nickleby, to whom relevancy is nothing, the whole of their past life is like an inexhaustible fairyland. Just as we take a rambling walk because we know that a district is beautiful, so they indulge a rambling mind because they know that a whole existence is interesting. A boy does not plunge into his future more romantically and at random than they plunge into their past.' Even the folds and stretches that our tired feet have left behind them become transfigured with exquisite beauty as we press courageously on and thread the labyrinth of life's long lane. The Present has a lovely way of wreathing an aureole about the brows of the Past. And even though the Present seems nothing but a dreary commonplace, the Future will do as much for her in God's good time. He maketh everything to be beautiful in its time; but it may not be the present time. To-morrow we shall see the glory of to-day. 'You always said my lane would turn,' wrote the 'Lady of the Decoration,' 'and it *has* turned into a broad road bordered by cherry-blossoms and wistaria.' It is always so. The birds in the hedges on either hand are singing that we really lose nothing that is behind by pressing bravely towards what lies before. All the loveliness of the lane is ours, even though we have nearly reached the end.

> Grow old along with me!
> The best is yet to be,
> The last of life, for which the first was made.
> Our times are in His hand,
> Who saith, A whole I planned.
> Youth shows but half; trust God; see all, nor be afraid.

II

A TONIC OF BIG THINGS

IMMENSITY is magnificent medicine. That is one reason—if we may let the cat out of the bag—why the doctors send us to the seaside. We forget the tiddley-winking in the contemplation of the tremendons. We lose life's shallow worries in the vision of unplumbed depths. Those who have read Mrs. Barclay's *Rosary* will remember that, in the crisis of her life, the heroine, the Hon. Jane Champion, determined to consult her physician, Sir Deryck Brand. And, after having realized the fearful strain to which his poor patient's nerves had been subjected, he exclaimed: 'Here is a prescription for you! *See a few big things!*' He urged her to go out west, and see the stupendous Falls of Niagara, to go out east and see the Great Pyramid. 'Go for the big things,' he said; 'you will like to remember, when you are bothering about pouring water in and out of tea-cups, "Niagara is flowing still!"'

All of which is, of course, very excellent. It is

the word we need. The tendency of life is to drift among small things—small anxieties, small pleasures, small ideas, and small talk. He is a very wise physician indeed who can prescribe for us a tonic of big things. In the course of that long struggle in his own life which reflects itself in Christian's lengthy pilgrimage to the Cross, John Bunyan enters in his autobiography two records that are worthy of frequent observation. I quote, of course, from *Grace Abounding*: 'While I was thus afflicted with the fears of my own damnation,' he says, 'there were two things would make me wonder. One was, when I saw old people hunting after the things of this life, as if they should live here always; the other was, when I found professors much distressed and cast down when they met with outward losses. Lord, thought I, what ado is here about such little things as these!'

That is the point: 'Such little things as these!' We are like the pebbles on the beach. It is not easy to keep among the big ones at the top—the big ones that feel the laughing caress of every wave and the lovely radiance of every sunbeam. The tendency is to get shaken down among the small shingle underneath. But we are forgetting the other record from the inner life of Bunyan: 'Upon a day the good providence of God called me to Bedford, to

work at my calling, and in one of the streets of that
town I came where there were three or four poor
women sitting at a door, in the sun, talking about the
things of God. I heard, but understood not, for
they were far above, out of my reach. Their talk
was about a new birth, the work of God in their
hearts; they talked how God had visited their souls
with His love in the Lord Jesus, and with what
words and promises they had been refreshed, com-
forted, and supported.'

These two keynotes, the one taken from the first
quotation, and the other from the second, are worth
repeating. 'Such little things as these!' 'The
things of God—far above—out of my reach.' The
soul of the poor tinker was tired of the microscopic
and hungry for the majestic. He craved 'a tonic of
big things,' and the talk of the four poor women
sitting in the sun was like a banquet to his famished
spirit.

The thing has its parallel everywhere. To take
one of the most familiar of all our religious classics,
it occurs in John Wesley's Journal. We all remem-
ber how pitifully weary the great Methodist apostle
became of the crowd of small men who buzzed about
him with a multitude of small concerns. And we
have all felt the glow of his delight when he found
some kindred spirit with whom he could freely con-

verse on the great themes of the Christian gospel.
There are times when we get so tired of the plain;
we love to get among the mountains. The soul
makes its own pilgrimage among great, rugged,
snow-clad ranges, along whose tracks and passes she
never loses her way. She loves the peaks that pierce
the sky; she enjoys 'the tonic of big things.'

In Lord Morley's *magnum opus* he reproduces
one of Mr. Gladstone's letters, in which the great
statesman tells of a visit to Dr. Chalmers. And by
nothing was Mr. Gladstone more impressed than by
the utter incapacity of Chalmers to indulge in small
talk. He simply lived among mountains. Every-
thing about Chalmers was massive, monumental,
magnificent. Who that has read it can ever forget
his historic utterance before the General Assembly
of the Church of Scotland, when he explained his
change of views on the subject of ministerial prepa-
ration? He explained, first of all, the change that
had come over his own spiritual life. 'I was wrong,
sir!' he cried, 'strangely blinded that I was! What,
sir, is the object of mathematical science? MAGNI-
TUDE, and the proportion of magnitude. But *then,*
sir, I had forgotten *two magnitudes*—I thought not
of the littleness of time, I recklessly thought not of
the greatness of eternity!' That word 'magnitude'
was characteristic of the man. And it profoundly

impressed Mr. Gladstone as being characteristic of his conversation. When only tiny themes presented themselves, the doctor was as silent as the Sphinx. 'He had nothing to say,' says Mr. Gladstone; 'he was exactly like the Duke of Wellington, who said of himself that he had no small talk. His whole mind was always full of some great subject, and he could not deviate from it.' 'Chalmers never wasted time on small topics,' Dr. Donald Fraser tells us in his biography, 'if he could find a man fit to enter on great matters.'

In the classical and memorable passage towards the end of the *Decline and Fall of the Roman Empire,* Gibbon describes the triumph of the most majestic masterpieces of Roman architecture. Huns, Goths, and Vandals had done their worst. The city had been sacked again and again; the hand of the iconoclast had been pitiless. Everything destructible had been ruthlessly destroyed; yet some things remained. They remained because they were not destructible; and those things were the big things. The fretwork and the fancy work, the delicate carvings and dainty ornamentations had fallen before the brutality of the Vandals; but the towering columns and colossal arches defied alike the teeth of time and the malice of the barbarian. The big things stand. 'Now abideth. . . .' It is ever so.

Every preacher knows that it is the great themes that hold the field; and they hold the field simply because the people, tired to death of trifles, need 'a tonic of big things.' The preacher of small subjects is doomed. The Canadian *Presbyterian* commented recently on the farewell services of a minister who was closing a two years' ministry. A venerable member of his congregation, in bidding his pastor a tearful 'good-bye,' remarked: 'Well, sir, I am sorry to see you go. I never had but one objection to you: your preaching was always *too horizontal!*' That is the worst of small things, however prettily presented. A multitude of grains of sand, however beautiful each separate grain may be in itself, only makes a desert after all; and there is no blinking the fact that deserts are not popular institutions. People don't like living in deserts; they like altitudes, magnitudes, infinitudes; they revel in the ruggedness of the ranges. 'I almost envy some of these good people who can stand in the middle of one of their prayers and touch all four sides.' It is the 'Lady of the Decoration' who is speaking; and she goes on: 'They know what they want, and are satisfied when they get it; but I want the moon and the stars and the sun thrown in!' Yes; our poor humanity needs 'a tonic of big things.'

The preacher must take note. The pulpit is the place for magnificent verities. It is the home of immensities, infinities, eternities. 'We must preach more upon the great texts of the Scriptures,' says Dr. Jowett, 'we must preach on those tremendous passages whose vastnesses almost terrify us as we approach them.'

Professor Henry Drummond was once sailing along the west coast of Africa. His deck companions were four men, no one of whom could understand the other; they spake in divers tongues. But at last one produced a Bible. The second hurried to his cabin and appeared with his; then the third, and then the fourth. By a stroke of genius, the first opened his at the third chapter of John's Gospel, and the great sixteenth verse. The others opened theirs, and pointed with their fingers to the place; and the glow on their faces was an eloquent language in itself. Men can see the mountain-peak over a multitude of intervening obstacles. And no obstacle of race or language, rank or station, can preclude men from the fellowship of life's immensities. 'They shall cry unto the Lord, and He shall send them a Saviour, *and a great one.*' Everything in the gospel is 'a tonic of big things.'

III

SERMONS AND SANDWICHES

IT was the church anniversary. On the Sunday there were special sermons, solemn praise, and stately anthems. Everything was inspiring, impressive, sublime. On the Monday there were sandwiches, cream puffs, and jam-tarts. The steaming urns imparted a genial glow to the spirits of the guests, for waves of laughter rippled and broke through the hum of friendly chatter. I had taken part in the solemn services of the Sunday, and had been asked to speak at the tea-meeting on the Monday. I drew aside to collect my thoughts. But my thoughts politely, but firmly, declined to be collected. They insisted on propounding to me this arresting conundrum—tell us, they clamoured, the philosophical connexion between the *sermons* of yesterday and the *sandwiches* of to-day. What relation exists between singing and scones? What fellowship hath religion with revelry? Why follow the sacred worship of the Lord's Day with a carnival of confectionery?

I took my Bible from my pocket, and had not

to search far before I came upon a clue. On one
of the very earliest pages of the sacred records I
lit upon a significant statement. It occurs at a
crisis in Hebrew history. It was a time of wealthy
revelation and divine illumination. Here it is:
'They saw God, and did eat and drink.' There
you have revelation and revelry side by side. There
you have the secret of all worship and the germ of
all tea-meetings. 'They saw God'—that is the prin-
ciple of the *sermon*; 'and did eat and drink'—that
is the principle of the *sandwich*. What more could
I desire? Yet I read on, and, to my amazement, I
found these two great principles running side by
side, like a pair of white horses perfectly matched,
through the entire volume. The sandwich was
never far from the sermon.

In the Old Testament all the stirring seasons
of spiritual elevation and national enlightenment
were *Feasts*—the Feast of Pentecost, the Feast of
Tabernacles, the Feast of Passover, the Feast of
Trumpets, the Feast of Dedication, and so on.
Revelation blends with revelry. The chapter that
tells of Israel's redemption from Egypt by the
shedding of blood—a classic of revelation—tells
also, in precise and graphic detail, of the eating of
the lamb. The passage that tells how Elijah saw the
angel tells also how the angel said, 'Arise and eat!'

'And, behold, a cake baken on the coals, and a cruse of water.'

The sandwich principle keeps pace with the sermon principle. Revelry goes hand in hand with revelation. The tea-meeting is never far from the special services. But the most revealing element in the ancient economy was its law of sacrifice. The old dispensation crystallized itself in the altar. And here we all sit at the feet of Professor Robertson Smith. He made this theme peculiarly his own. And he fearlessly affirms that we cannot understand that solemn and striking symbol of patriarchal faith unless we grasp the fact that the altar was first of all a table. 'This,' he says, 'is the key to the whole subject of sacrifice, and the basis of all Semitic covenants. When the two parties have eaten of the same victim, and thus become participants in a common life, a living bond of union is established between them, and they are no longer enemies, but brothers.' Here, then, are the two laws—the law of the sermon and the law of the sandwich, the principle of revelation and the principle of revelry —in closest juxtaposition at the very climax of the old world's illumination.

Crossing the border-line into the New Testament, the same singular conjunction is everywhere. 'This beginning of miracles did Jesus in Cana of Galilee, and manifested forth His glory.' The revelation was a revelry. It was at a marriage feast. Later miracles followed the same line—the feeding of four thousand, the feeding of five thousand, and so on. Loaves and fishes—the representation of the sandwich—were never far from the most revealing sermons of the Son of Man. And even when, after His resurrection, He deigns to show Himself to His astounded fishermen, He feeds them. 'And they saw a fire of coals, and fish laid thereon, and bread.' Revelation and revelry are together still. And just as the Old Testament reaches its natural climax in the Altar of Sacrifice, so the New Testament reaches its culminating revelation in the Table of the Lord. There 'we see God, and do eat and drink.' The two principles join hand in hand. And even when the Great Revealer spoke of heaven, these two thoughts were always in His mind. Heaven is a place of revelation and of revelry. There the pure in heart see God; and there we sit down at the Marriage Supper of the Lamb. Men often do things, as the swallows do, under the guidance of some sure instinct, yet without detecting, or even desiring, any explanation of their odd behaviour. It is thus that the Church has wedded her revelries to her revelations. She has rightly set the sandwich over against the sermon. The union is indissoluble. The solemn service and the social meal are inseparable. These two hath God joined together.

Now in these two elements I find my bond of brotherhood with the holiest and the lowliest. Among the angels and archangels and all the company of the heavenly host I know not what seraphic spirits may burn. But I know that there is no altitude higher than this to which they can attain—they see God! But so do I. Then they and I are brothers. In the splendid revelations of Christian worship we stand allied to the holiest in the height. And in eating and drinking, on the other hand, we are kinned to the lowliest. I watch the birds as they fly. It seems to me that they live in one element, and I in another; we have nothing in common. I watch the rabbit as he shyly peeps from his burrow. How far. removed his life from mine! I watch the trout as they flash and dart in the shades and shallows of the stream. There is no point of fellowship between them and me. But wait! The rabbit sits upon his haunches nibbling at a blade of grass, on which a dewdrop glistens. He eats and drinks! So do I. The bird flutters down from the bough to seize a morsel on the lawn. He eats and drinks! So do I. The fish come darting up the stream to

devour the gnats that, in trying to escape the
birds, have fallen upon the glassy surface. They
eat and drink! So do I. If the sermon allies
me to angels and to seraphs, the sandwich allies
me to all things furry and feathered and finny.
When we were prattlers our nurses used to amuse
us with fantastic pictures of lions and storks and
ants and dolphins and men all sitting down, cheek
by jowl, at the same table.

Later on we despised the old print as a furious
freak of some farcical fancy. But now we know
that it was nothing of the kind. It was a severely
accurate delineation of the real and sober truth.
Indeed, it was less than the truth, for no superhuman
guests were there. The universe is a banqueting-
table. That sage old friar—Francis d'Assisi—was
within the mark, after all, when he addressed the
creatures as Brother Hare, Sister Lark, Brother
Wolf, and so on. The *sermon* element brings me
into intimate and fraternal relationship with all the
flaming hosts above. The *sandwich* element brings
me into league with the tigers, and the tomtits,
and the trout. The special services of anniversary
Sunday, and the tea-meeting of the Monday, set
forth in harmonious combination the breadth and
catholicity of man's holiest and lowliest brother-
hoods.

But the instinct of the tea-meeting tells me yet
one other thing. I see now that I have misinter-
preted the majesty of God. 'It is the pathetic fate
of Deity,' says Pascal, 'to be everlastingly misunder-
stood.' I had always supposed that the glory of
God was embarrassing, bewildering, dazzling! I
had thought of it as repelling, terrifying, paralysing!
But now I see that it is nothing of the kind. 'They
saw God, and did eat and drink.' Even a cat
will not eat in a strange house, nor a bird in a
strange cage. Eating and drinking are symbols of
familiarity. We feel at home. We bring our friends
to our tables that they may realize their welcome.
My ugly thought of God was a caricature, a parody,
an insult. Man was made for God, and only finds
his perfect poise in His presence. To see God
is to eat and drink—to be perfectly, peacefully,
reverently, restfully, delightfully at home.

'"I have served God, and feared Him with all
my heart," says poor Rufus Webb in Miss Ellen
Thorneycroft Fowler's *Fuel of Fire.*

'"That may be, but you have never *loved* nor
trusted Him!" replied the minister.

'The dying man lay silent for a few minutes, with
closed eyes. Then he opened them again, and said:
"I wonder if you are right, and I have misjudged
Him all these years?"

' "I am sure of it."

' "And do you think He will pardon me that also, in addition to my many other sins?"

' "I am sure of it," repeated the vicar, "although it is hard, even for Him, to be misjudged by those whom He loves; there are few things harder." '

It is even so. I heard the solemn pathos of this philosophy jingled out in the clatter of the cups and the spoons at the tea-meeting. 'A glorious high throne is the place of *our sanctuary*.' It is not repelling; it is restful. He who sees God eats and drinks. The sandwiches naturally follow the sermons. 'If any man hear My voice I will come in to him, and will sup with him, and he with Me.'

IV

THE CHALLENGE OF THE HEIGHTS

ONE of the world's most intrepid mountaineers, Mr. George D. Abraham, has published a record of his adventures. His experiences have quite a startling significance for life at all points. Much that he says is as bracing as those stinging breezes that hurled the hail in his face as he invaded the snowy solitudes and carved the first path over slippery glaciers. He reminds us, for example, that nobody has yet stood on the roof of the world. The real sky-piercers have never yet been climbed. On almost every continent the loftiest summits wrap their clouds about them and stand defiant and triumphant. They have never felt the proud heel of a conqueror.

It is good, both for our humiliation and for our inspiration, that we should lay that pregnant record to heart. In days when bewildering inventions and sensational discoveries leap from our newspapers with every plate of porridge, it is as well that we should be made to feel that, after all, we have only been toying with trivialities. Our grandchildren will ransack some old chest or drawer, and drag from its seclusion an old illustrated paper of, let us say, the year 1912. They will scream with furious glee as they scan the photographs of the aeroplanes and automobiles which so hugely tickled our own vanity; and then, as they read the accompanying letter-press, and feel the pulsations of our pride, they will awaken all the echoes with their boisterous shouts of laughter.

It is very humiliating; and yet, after all, surely it is powerfully invigorating too. Who does not feel that life holds a new meaning for him as he reflects that there are dizzy heights which have stood in naked and awful silence from the foundation of the world? Their desolate grandeur is waiting for the pilgrim feet of a pioneer. Who does not experience a thrill as he remembers that it is possible for us to break all the records of the ages and burst upon the vacancies that ache for conquest?

Mr. Abraham contends that the first man to ascend Mount Everest will be a greater benefactor of his race than a successful polar explorer. It may be humiliating to be reminded that we have not discovered everything. But it would be simply crushing if we were assured that nothing remained to be discovered. The tang of these icy winds that sweep down these untrodden slopes taunts the imagination and challenges the enthusiasms of the world. All the greatest heights have yet to be climbed. It is grand! All the sweetest songs have yet to be sung; all the noblest poems have yet to be penned; all the greatest books have yet to be written; all the finest sermons have yet to be preached; all the truest lives have yet to be lived; all the most heroic exploits have yet to be achieved. The whole wide world, with its restless millions, waits to be conquered. India, China, Africa, South America, spacious continents, crowded countries, cannibal islands and coral reefs, all wait—as the peaks wait for the pathfinder—for the beautiful feet of those triumphant mountaineers whose coming will precipitate the conquest of the ages. The challenge of the heights is in our ears; it stirs our blood; it fires our fancy. It is a day for girding our loins for heroic enterprise. The pinnacles beckon and the topmost crags are calling. We must quit the pine-clad valleys; we must go. The Golden Age has still to be ushered in.

Then, again, Mr. Abraham conclusively demonstrates that, on the dizzy Alpine tracks, no man liveth to himself. He insists on the social element in mountaineering. The heights must be scaled, not by individuals, but by parties, and every member of the party is part and parcel of every other member. No brotherhood could be more real, more practical, more imperative. Sometimes the members of the expedition are roped together; but in any case the tie is there. In negotiating a difficult pass, in clambering up a perilous face, or in attempting a forbidding ascent, it is the weakest member of the expedition whom all other members must consider. His failure would be the failure of all. The golden rule is nowhere so clamant as among the crags of the summit. Every task that presents itself has to be faced with a full recognition of its suitability to the capabilities of each member of the fraternity. The slipping of the feeblest foot might easily jeopardize the lives of all. That is for ever and for ever the lesson of the heights. It is only in life's rarer and more intense atmospheres that we see it so clearly. The murky mists of the valley often obscure the fact that we are, in deed and in truth, members one of another.

In his great chapter on 'The Evolution of Language,' Drummond shows that a law like this operates in the animal world. 'One of the earliest devices hit upon,' he says, 'was the principle of co-operation. The deer formed themselves into herds, the monkeys into troops, the birds into flocks, the wolves into packs, the bees into hives, and the ants into colonies.' And the brilliant doctor goes on to show how it works out: 'Here,' he says, 'is a herd of deer, scattered, as they love to be, in a string a quarter of a mile long. Every animal in the herd not only shares the physical strength of all the rest, but their powers of observation.'

The very beasts of the field are members one of another, and know it. But the finest and most graceful illustration of this social law—the strength of the strongest passing as a heritage to the feeblest —occurs in *The Pilgrim's Progress*. ' "Alas!" cried poor Mr. Feeble-mind, "I want a suitable companion; you are all so lusty and strong; but I, as you see, am weak. I choose, therefore, rather to come behind, lest by reason of my many infirmities I should be both a burthen to myself and to you. I am, as I said, a man of a weak and a feeble mind, and shall be offended and made weak at that which others can bear. I shall like no laughing; I shall like no gay attire; I shall like no unprofitable questions. Nay, I am so weak a man as to be offended with that which others have a liberty to do. I do not yet know all the truth; I am a very ignorant Christian man; sometimes, if I hear some rejoice in the Lord, it troubles me because I cannot do so too. It is with me as it is with a weak man among the strong, or as with a sick man among the healthy, or as a lamp despised, so that I know not what to do." "But, brother," said Mr. Greatheart, "I have it in commission to comfort the feeble-minded, and to support the weak. You must needs go along with us; we will wait for you, and we will lend you our help; we will deny ourselves of some things, both opinionated and practical, for your sake; we will not enter into doubtful disputations before you; we will be made all things to you, rather than that you shall be left behind." '

The Pathfinder, the Professor, and the Puritan all agree, therefore, in making it abundantly clear that no man liveth to himself, and no man dieth to himself. 'Wherefore,' says the most sure-footed of all our mountaineers, 'take heed to them that are weak. It is good neither to eat flesh, nor to drink wine, nor anything whereby thy brother stumbleth.' The echo that we have heard comes to us from the Alps and the Himalayas; but the voice that awoke that echo is from a greater height. It spake from Mount Sinai, from Mount Sion, from the eternal altitudes. It is the voice of God.

A third striking thing our mountaineer has to say. He emphasizes the astonishing fact that the vast majority of Alpine fatalities occur on the easy tracks. The steep and narrow passes, where the brain reels, where the foothold is precarious, and where the poise of the body is difficult, clamour loudly for special care. But the easy tracks have a peril of their own. 'Claudius Clear,' in a suggestive article, demonstrated the fact that, although we commonly regard youth as the essential period of moral peril, the most disastrous collapses have been on the part of men and women in middle life. We acquire a certain fatal contempt for temptation which is ultimately our undoing. We have edged our way with trembling caution along the most slender shelves, beside perpendicular cliffs, and above yawning abysses; and then we fling ourselves with a reckless stride along the broader tracks. We scorn the danger. Are we not noted climbers—ministers, officers, teachers, saints of ripe or mellow maturity? Thinking that we stand fast, we take no heed lest we fall. We become the victims of the easy track at the last. It is cruelly anomalous, but it is tragically true, that many a man's conscience is less sensitive as to the minor moralities of life after twenty years of Christian service than during the first months of his religious experience. He slips now where he stood fast then. He has become too confident to be cautious, and has grown tired of being careful. That way lies disaster.

We feel very much obliged to Mr. Abraham.

We never expect, in this life, to follow **him on** his
vigorous pilgrimages towards virgin peaks. We
can only gaze at his snowy summits admiringly
and wistfully. But his adventures read like al-
legories; his suggestions sound like sermons. The
analogies, however unintentional, are too arresting
to be shunned; the parallelisms, however uncon-
scious, too striking to be avoided. We have fol-
lowed this trusty guide by granite and glacier, midst
snow and ice, and have caught a vision of more
radiant purity, gleaming on loftier pinnacles, and
bathed in the golden glory of a lovelier sunrise.
And those beckoning heights have challenged us to
press with new vigour towards the triumphs for
which all the ages have been struggling, to reach
out hands of dearer brotherhood to the comrades
who share our pilgrimage, and to exercise a greater
vigilance as we tread life's treacherous easy tracks.
It is so easy to fail of life's loftiest altitudes; so easy
to forget the partner of one's toil and travel; so
wofully easy to be overtaken by desolating calamity
through a false step on the easy track, after all.
After all!

V

THE FURNITURE-VAN

I AM writing in April. The month moves on its way amidst a wealthy cluster of associations. It opens with a festival of folly. The Englishman invariably connects its coming with welcome thoughts of the cuckoo and the crocus. In our Australian minds it stands related to the rustle of autumn leaves. It is the month of homeward yearning, too, for all exiles. There be many that say, as Browning said:

> Oh to be in England
> Now that April's there!
> 'And whoever wakes in England
> Sees, some morning, unaware,
> That the lowest boughs and the brushwood sheaf
> Round the elm-tree bole are in tiny leaf,
> While the chaffinch sings on the orchard bough
> In England—now.

April brings, too, more often than not, the tender pathos of Good Friday, and the exquisite triumph of Easter. But there is one home to which these chastened joys make no appeal, for to the door of the Australian Methodist parsonage April brings only the furniture-van. We have been engaged in

saying sorrowful farewells to ministerial neigh-
bours with whom we have worked side by side
through pleasant years of comradeship. And now,
without any indication that their work is finished,
like plants torn up when in full bloom, they must
move on.

It is this that has set us thinking. Indeed, it has
set Methodism • thinking. The whole question of
ministerial movement is beset by problems that have
made wiser heads than ours to ache. It is true, on
the one hand, that the itinerary system is being
eyed, not without envy, by the statesmen of other
churches. Here, for example, in the latest issue of
The Church Family Newspaper, is a leading article
suggesting the adoption by the Church of England
of a modified Methodism. Presbyterian assemblies
have long been discussing it, and Baptists and Con-
gregationalists have sometimes cast shy but wistful
glances in the same direction. And yet—and yet, on
the other hand, two things are clear. The *first* is
that Methodism itself is coming to regard the system
as open to review. I have known large city churches
apply for registration as central missions in order
that they may stand outside the pale of the
itinerary system. And I have known small country
churches plead that they might retain their status
as home missions rather than be dragged into the

sweep of the system. The *second* fact is that every minister who has stayed in one place long enough to marry the girls and boys that he kissed when he came, knows that his most regal influence came to him in the years that followed the fifth. It is then that the best work is done. The minister has won a personal, in addition to a merely official authority. His name is graven in the very hearts of his people, and he speaks in their homes with the voice of a king.

But let me hasten to say that I am writing to challenge no system, and to advocate no system. All these things are in the melting-pot; and the churches will be wise if they watch each other closely, confer with each other frankly, and profit by each other's sagacity and experience. Yet one thing I do most unhesitatingly affirm, and it is for that irresistible affirmation that I am contending now. It is this: a ministerial removal should *never* be mechanical. It is a crisis of the soul—perhaps of many souls. It is a thing to be undertaken only after strong crying and tears. I like to recall the searchings of heart that marked a ministerial resignation a century or so ago. Everybody knows the circumstances under which poor old John Fawcett wrote 'Blest be the tie that binds.' And, at about the same time, Andrew Fuller spent two years in

most terrible anguish of soul whilst he tried to de-
termine whether or not it was his duty to leave his
little flock at Soham. 'It seems as if the church
and I should break each other's hearts,' he wrote.
'I think, after all, if I go from them, it must be
in my coffin.' His agony of mind led Dr. Ryland
to remark that 'men who fear not God would risk
an empire with fewer searchings of heart than it
cost Andrew Fuller to leave a little church, hardly
containing forty members besides himself and his
wife.'

And, indeed, there is no need to limit the scope
of this chapter to manses and parsonages. The same
principle holds good of every removal. The ten-
dency of young nations is to regard the furniture-
van flippantly. A century ago, the removal of an
English family from one village to another was
regarded as a social tragedy through all the country-
side. A man worked for his master because his
father had worked for his master's father, and his
grandfather for his master's grandfather. And it
never occurred to him that some social cataclysm
might prevent his grandchildren from serving his
master's grandchildren. All that has changed.
That day is as dead as the moa and the dodo. The
temper of the time has altered. We hail a furniture-
van nowadays with almost as light a heart as we hail

a hansom cab. In his *Gamekeeper at Home* Richard
Jefferies, the naturalist, maintains that this very fact
has had a good deal to do with the sharp accentua-
tion of our industrial troubles. The old intimate
and almost sacred relationship between employer
and employé, fortified by associations sanctified by
several generations, has broken down; and its col-
lapse has paved the way for all our modern embroil-
ments and agitations.

Yes, there is no doubt about it, we overwork the
furniture-van. Its axles are too hot. Old Daniel
Quorm comes to mind. 'I do often see it, friends!'
said Dan'l, 'I've watched it for years. Here's a
young fellow doin' good in the Sunday school and
other ways, promising to be a useful man when we
old folks are gone home. But somebody sends down
word that he can make half a crown a week more
wages in London. That's enough. No prayer about
it; no askin' the Lord what He do see. No thinkin'
about the Lord's work. "I must get on," he says,
and he says it so pious as if it was one o' the ten
commandments—but 'tisn't, friends, 'tisn't, 'though
you do hear it so often!'

Over against Daniel Quorm let us set Dr. Alex-
ander Whyte. In his lecture on 'Treasure Hid in
the Field' the doctor touches on this very matter,
and tells of a lovely experience. 'An old office-

bearer of this very congregation,' he says, 'told me, long ago, how he had lately summoned a conference of his whole household in order to make a great family choice and decision. He put it to his wife, and to his sons, and to his daughters, whether he would build a house for them away out of Edinburgh, with a park and a garden and stables, or whether he would buy a house in the city so as still to be near this church, and so as to let his family continue to sit under Dr. Candlish's ministry. And the eyes of that old elder glistened with joy when he told me that he had determined on a house within reach of the pulpit to which he owed his own soul and the souls of his children. His wife had been in Dr. Candlish's ladies' class. Things like that do not happen every day.'

Dr. Whyte is right. They do not. We are too fond of the furniture-van. We ought to regard it in the same category as the world and the flesh and the devil. The number of transfers granted to members leaving one church for another would make our grandsires turn in their graves, whilst the multitude of those who are entered as having 'moved away,' one church's loss being no other church's gain, is appalling. They have *moved away*, that is all. The furniture-van has done its deadly work. Father, mother, lads and lasses have moved away from church and Sunday school, from societies and classes, from useful services and helpful charities and happy ministries; they have moved away—to what? Church secretaries might often mournfully and truthfully enter in the 'Remarks' column of the church-roll the 'Lay of the Lost Leader':

> Just for a handful of silver he left us,
> Just for a riband to stick in his coat!

Nobody, of course, is so dreamy and unpractical as to suggest that church connexions should never be ruptured in order to secure commercial promotion or industrial preferment. That is not the point. The iniquity is with those who order the furniture-van before such considerations have been duly weighed. If a man sees the beckoning hand, he must go on; and, so long as he is clear that his move is a move nearer to the realization of life's ultimate purpose, the furniture-van may be as idyllic a vehicle for him as a chariot and horses of fire.

But there is a 'moving away' that is worse still. Paul assures the Christians at Colossae that their Lord shall present them holy and unblamable and unreprovable if they be not *moved away* from the hope of the gospel. That is sorrow's crown of sorrow—life's culminating climax of tragedy—to be *moved away* from the hope of the gospel. Wherever the furniture-van may take our chairs and tables, our hearts must always abide in the same place. In an age of shifting and of drifting we must make it the loftiest science of life to dwell in the secret place of the Most High and to abide under the shadow of the Almighty. In the immutable Rock of Ages the soul must wisely build her nest. 'Be not moved away'! Surely, if church secretaries are sometimes tempted to inscribe the 'Lay of the Lost Leader' against certain names on the membership roll, it is pardonable to fancy the very angels, from their higher knowledge, writing sadly against other names, '*Moved away*—moved away from the hope of the gospel.' It is the Dirge of a Lost Soul!

Mr. Young, of Jedburgh, used to tell a story of old Janet, who, in her lonely hut on the Scottish moor, was dying at last. She breathed heavily and painfully. Her brown old Bible lay open on the counterpane. The minister came just in time. 'And hoo is't wi' ye the noo, Janet?' he inquired, bending over her wrinkled countenance. Her face was radiant. 'It's a' weel, it's bonnie,' she cried; 'but, mon, I'm *a wee confused wi' the flittin'*!' Happy are all they who, in that last solemn removal, know no more poignant anguish than the mere flutter and flurry of the process!

VI

ON THE WISDOM OF CONDUCTING ONE'S OWN FUNERAL

MARK TWAIN more than once makes merry at the lugubrious and fantastic conception of a man mourning at his own funeral. In these passages the genial humorist is not at his best. He misses the true inwardness of things. There is nothing in actual experience more common and nothing more pathetic than for a man to occupy the position of chief mourner at his own burial. We have often read the touching records of missionaries on the islands, who are compelled to act as grave-diggers and chaplains at the funerals of their own wives and children. And quite recently we heard of a stricken and lonely woman, in an ocean solitude, who was called to nerve herself to perform the same melancholy offices at the burial of her husband. But life holds an even deeper pathos. It is the tragic experience of every man who rightly reads the riddle of life to preside, perhaps more than once, at his own obsequies. He looks tearfully down upon the plate upon which his own name and age are inscribed, and says, deliberately and bravely, 'Ashes to ashes, dust to dust.' Lord Dufferin has told us that he owes his very life to a vivid dream in the course of which he seemed to be a mourner at his own funeral. Many a man owes far more than life itself not to a mere dream, but to the actual experience.

The process occurs, for instance, in the choice of a profession. Here and there a man feels that he must follow a certain line, and that no other is even thinkable. But with most men the trail is not so clearly blazed. A man decides to be a builder, but he feels that he would have made a very respectable banker. Or he resolves on being a minister, but he feels at the same time that he could easily have distinguished himself as a barrister. In such cases, if he be wise, the builder will straightway bury the banker that is in him, and the minister will pronounce the solemn words of committal over the grave of the barrister. The builder who is perpetually hankering after a teller's desk will never build anything better than huts or hovels—even for himself. And the minister who is for ever casting envious eyes at a barrister's chambers will never catch the rapture that Christ's true ministers may know.

That is a great story which Professor Herkless

tells us in his Life of Francis d'Assisi. On the one hand Francis longed to be a friar and to dedicate himself to poverty and pilgrimage. On the other hand he loved a sweet and noble and gracious woman. He wrestled with his alternatives, and at length, through an agony of tears, he chose the cloak and the cowl. But still the lovely face haunted him by cloister and by shrine. And one radiant moonlit night, when the earth was wrapped in snow, the brethren of the monastery saw him rise at dead of night. He went out into the grounds, and, in the silvery moonlight, fashioned, out of the snow, images of wife and children and servants. He arranged them in a circle, and sat with them, and, giving rein to his fancy, tasted for one delicious hour the ecstasies of hearth and home, the joys of life and love. Then, solemnly rising, he kissed them all a tearful and a final farewell, renounced such raptures for ever, and re-entered the convent. That night Francis the friar buried himself. He read his own funeral service. He had made his choice; and, in order that his life might not be clogged by the haunting images of dead possibilities, the man who had decided to be a friar buried everything except the friar. Indeed, the Roman Church draws the most impressive symbolism of its dedication from this source. Lamartine tells us

of Madame Roland's visit to a French convent.
'A novice took the veil during her residence there.
Her presentation at the entrance, her white veil,
her crown of roses, the sweet and soothing hymns
which directed her from earth to heaven, *the mortu-
ary cloth cast over her youthful and buried beauty
and over her palpitating heart,* made Madame
Roland shudder and overwhelmed her with tears.'

But there is no need to go beyond the pale
of Protestantism for our illustrations. The case
of F. W. Robertson of Brighton is very much to
the point. The love of arms ran in his very blood.
His grandfather, his father, and his brothers were
all soldiers. He himself had counted the slow years
that must drag by before he could wear the Queen's
uniform. But at last the time came, and he found
himself, to his intense delight, appointed to the
Third Dragoon Guards, and almost simultaneously
there came the call to the ministry. Then the
struggle in the dark, and, finally, the great decision.
Robertson stripped off the brilliant uniform, laid
aside his sword, entered the ministry, and from
that time forth never looked back. The first
service he conducted, he conducted all alone. It
was the burial of the soldier in him. And, before
burying him, he stripped from the soldier all his
military virtues—endurance, discipline, courage—

and transferred them to the equipment of the minister.

If our years were allotted to us in the generous fashion which some of the patriarchs seem to have enjoyed, a man might find some opportunity for trying his hand at more avocations than one. As it is, however, the time is short. At seventy a man only begins to feel that he knows his work. There is no time for tinkering with many things or for trifling with one. The very brevity of life clamours for concentration and economy. We have all read the affecting and informing and heart-searching correspondence of Dr. Marcus Dods. No man sounded the very depths of life's innermost experiences more terribly than did he. He felt called to be a minister. He buried every other inclination and possibility. Then came years of neglect and rejection. No congregation would call him. But, with a courage never excelled on a battle-field, he held on. He looked wistfully at the graves in which he had buried his earlier fancies. But he would allow no resurrection. And at last came recognition and reward. And out of that agonizing experience he wrote on the economy of life, and he deserves to be listened to with bated breath. 'Every man,' the doctor says, 'as he grows into life, finds he must employ such an economy on his own account. He is pressed to occupy positions or to engage in work which will prevent him from achieving the purpose for which nature has fitted him. He is offered promotion which seems attractive and has its advantages; but he declines it, because it would divert him from his chosen aim. Continually men spoil their life by want of concentration. They are greatly tempted to do so, for the public foolishly concludes that, because a man does one thing well, he can do everything well; and he who has written a good history is straightway asked to sit in Parliament, or the man whose scholarship and piety have been conspicuous is offered preferment which calls for the exercise of wholly different qualities.'

The theme might, of course, be amplified infinitely. It is the central thought of the gospel. There are times when men sigh, with the speaker in Tennyson's *Maud*:

> Ah, for a man to arise in me,
> That the man I am may cease to be!

And Jesus meets such men on their own ground. He offers a new life. 'Ye must be *born* again'! He says. And the birth within me of the man He means me to be necessarily implies the burial within me of the man I have actually been. The vocabulary of the death-bed and the grave-side was constantly on the lips of Paul. Again and again he told

the Christians of Europe and of Asia the story of
his own death and burial.   Almost all his auto-
biographical references are obituary notices.   He
had been crucified with Christ, he would say, and
he implored his hearers to reckon themselves as
dead and buried too.

Yes, it is good for the builder to bury the banker
that he might have been.   It is good for Paul to bury
the Saul that he had been.   But there is one man
within us, whom we are most strongly tempted to
bury, to whose funeral we must never, *never* go.   He
is the man of our ideal; the man of our prayers;
the man we fain would be.   There are no sadder
lines in English poetry than those of William Wat-
son:

> So on our souls the visions rise
>   Of that fair life we never led:
> They flash a splendour past our eyes,
>   We start, and they are fled;
> They pass and leave us with blank gaze,
> Resigned to our ignoble days.

We catch the fair vision of glorious possibilities;
but we shake our heads, like the rich young ruler,
and turn away sorrowful.   Oh the pity of it!
'Resigned to our ignoble days'!   The old world is
very weary with weeping over her troubles and
her tragedies; but she has never known anything
more inexpressibly mournful than that.

VII

OUR BETTER HALVES

MARRIAGE is simply an obvious and outstanding illustration of one of life's cardinal laws. The world is made up of pairs, and, like the sexes, those pairs are supplementary and complementary. I have two eyes. They are not in rivalry; each has its function. It is difficult for my right eye to discern the danger that approaches from the opposite direction. My left eye, therefore, stands sentinel on that side of my face. Each member of my body holds in charge powers that it is under obligation to exercise for the good of all its fellow members. The world is built on that plan. Examine, for proof of it, the list of exports and imports of any nation under the sun. As Cowper sings:

Wise to promote whatever end He means,
God opens fruitful Nature's various scenes;:
Each climate needs what other climes produce,
And offers something to the general use;
No land but listens to the common call,
And in return receives supplies from all.

216

In our silly habit of teaching half-truths, we tell our children that Australia belongs to Britain, that Algeria belongs to France, and that Java belongs to Holland. If we told them the *whole* truth they would learn that Britain belongs to Germany, and that France belongs to China, and that America belongs to Japan, and that every nation is an essential and complementary part of every other nation. And if we taught them the whole truth after that liberal fashion, they would grow up to beat their swords into ploughshares and their spears into pruning-hooks.

In precisely the same way every man holds in sacred charge certain gifts and graces which he is under solemn obligation to use for the general good. My next-door neighbour is my better half; I cannot do without him.

> He is rich where I am poor,
> And he supplies my wants the more
> As his unlikeness fitteth me.

The best possible illustration is, of course, Commander Verney L. Cameron's story of the two lepers he met in Central Africa. One had lost his hands, the other his feet. They established a farm together. The leper who had no hands, and who could not therefore scatter seed, carried his legless brother, who could not else have stirred, upon his back; and thus, each supplying the other's lack, they broke their ground, and sowed their seed, and reaped their crop.

Or go to Scotland. Everybody who has read that wealthiest of all northern biographies will remember the storm scene on the Highland loch. Dr. Norman Macleod was in a small boat with a boatman, some ladies, and 'a well-known ministerial brother, who was as conspicuous for his weak and puny appearance as Dr. Macleod was for his gigantic size and strength.' A fearful gale arose. The waves tossed the boat sky-high in their furious sport. The smaller of the two ministers was frightened out of his wits. He suggested that Dr. Macleod should pray for deliverance. The ladies eagerly seconded the devout proposal. But the breathless old boatman would have none of it. He instantly vetoed the scheme. 'Na, na!' he cried; 'let the wee mannie pray, but the big one maun tak' an oar if ye dinna a' want to be drooned!' The shrewd old Highlander was simply stating, in a crude way of his own, life's great supplementary law. Let us admire this principle of the big minister and the small minister, of the armless leper and the legless leper, each in his proper place, as it reveals itself in other fields. Every great movement furnishes evidence of the effective operation of this law.

Those who have studied carefully the story of the Reformation know how the powers of Luther and Melanchthon dovetailed into each other, and how beautifully each supplemented each. Differing from each other as widely as the poles, each seemed to supply precisely what the other lacked; and neither was quite sure of the wisdom of his own proposal until the sanction of the other had been obtained.

Macaulay has told us, concerning Charles Fox and Sir James Macintosh, that when Fox went to the desk and wrote, and Macintosh took to the platform and spoke, the cause they espoused seemed pitifully impotent; but when Macintosh seized the pen, and Fox mounted the platform, they were simply irresistible. They brought the whole country to their feet. Which, of course, is the story of the big minister and the wee minister over again. The gifts of each exactly supplemented those of the other. Each was the other's better half. And has not Lord Morley made us familiar with the fine record of Cobden and of Bright? 'They were,' he says, 'the complements of each other. Their gifts differed, so that one exactly covered the ground which the other was predisposed to leave comparatively untouched.'

The story of the grey friars and the black friars is another case in point. The followers of Francis exactly supplemented those of Dominic, and each order overtook the work which the other left undone. History teems with similar examples. The law of the better half is as wide in the sweep of its operations as the law of gravitation.

What ecclesiastical jealousies and theological bitternesses and ministerial heart-burnings would have been saved if even the best and saintliest of men had been swift to recognize the operation of this gracious principle! To say nothing of such shameful controversies as those between Calvinists and Lutherans, let us take as our example, a wordy conflict of but two centuries ago. We ministers read John Wesley's *Journal* and William Law's *Serious Call* on Saturday nights; and contact with such flaming enthusiasms makes our own hearts to burn within us as the great day of the week approaches. What piety, what passion, what prayerfulness we discover! All the chills of the week melt from our spirits as our souls warm themselves before these blazing fires! But we blush for our own revered spiritual masters when we recall the way in which these giants of the devout life treated each other. And, now that all the dust has settled, what is the truth? The simple fact is that Wesley was the very greatest preacher of his age, and Law was the very greatest religious writer.

'We see, now,' says a great writer, 'that William Law without John Wesley, as well as John Wesley without William Law, would have left the religious life and literature of the eighteenth century both weak, one-sided, and unsafe. Could they both have seen it, both were indispensable—John Wesley to complete William Law, and William Law to complete John Wesley.' Just so. *Could they both have seen it!* But the tragedy of it all is that they could not see it, and did not see it. We shall be wise men if, in sitting at their feet, we profit by the very blindness of our teachers. Each, had he only known it, was the other's better half.

There come to most of us weak or wicked moments, when we are apt to regard our more brilliant brethren as our enemies. We forget that we are members one of another, and that we need each other. What a story for tears is that which Dr. Alexander Whyte has told us of Thomas Shepard! It is a tale to be read on our knees. Thomas Shepard, as we all know, was an English Puritan, a Pilgrim Father, and the Founder of Harvard. But we did not all know that Thomas Shepard was a poor wretch of like passions with ourselves. He had, it seems, a brilliant ministerial neighbour. And his neighbour's sermons were printed on Saturdays in the *New England Gazette.* So, for that matter, were Shepard's. But his neighbour's sermons read well, and were popular. Shepard's read but indifferently, and were despised. And on one memorable Saturday a particularly brilliant and clever sermon appeared in the *Gazette.* Everybody read it, everybody talked of it, everybody praised it. And the praise of his neighbour was like fire in the bones and like gravel in the teeth of poor Thomas Shepard. It was gall and wormwood to his very soul. That Saturday the spirit of the old Puritan passed through the Garden of Gethsemane. When midnight came it found him still prostrate before God on the floor of his study. His whole frame was convulsed in an agony of sweat and tears, whilst his brilliant neighbour's clever sermon was still crushed and crumpled between his clasped hands. He wrestled, like Jacob, until the breaking of the day. He prayed until he had torn all bitterness and jealousy and hatred and ill-will out of his heart. And then, with calm and upturned face, he craved a blessing on his neighbour and on his neighbour's clever sermon. Thomas Shepard came to see that he and his neighbour belonged to each other. He was his neighbour's better half. Time has taken good care to vindicate Shepard. He is the friend of all of us, whilst we do not even know his neighbour's name. What Saturday nights, I say again,

we ministers have with Wesley and with Law!
How our hearts burn within us in their excellent
company! But what still more glorious Saturday
nights we might have had if only John Wesley or
William Law—or, better still, both of them—had
spent one Saturday night after the pattern of
Thomas Shepard's never-to-be-forgotten Saturday
night in New England! If only they, and all like
them, had wrestled with their bitterness until the
breaking of the day! The daybreak would have
revealed to each the noble face of a brother beloved.
For we are members one of another.

VIII

THE CONQUEST OF THE POLES

I HAVE just been over the *Fram*. Captain Amundsen, with his lieutenants, Messrs. Hassel and Wisting—both of whom accompanied their chief to the Pole—were as courteous and attentive as mortals could possibly be. They showed us all that there was to be seen, told us all that there was to be told, and assisted us in snapping everything that tempted our cameras. Nothing could have been more beautiful than the grace and modesty with which they were receiving, in the form of a perfect stream of congratulatory cablegrams, the plaudits of the world. It was good to walk the decks of the sturdy little vessel that holds the extraordinary record of having penetrated to the farthest north with Nansen and to the farthest south with Amundsen. We raise our hats to the heroic achievements of these hardy Norsemen. What memories rush to mind! What tales of dauntless courage and dogged endurance!

Our thoughts quit all their ordinary grooves and

224

plunge into fresh realms. We seem to leave the
solar system far behind us, and to invade a new
universe as we lean against these beaten bulwarks
and give ourselves to retrospection. And here, at
least, there are no more worlds to conquer. Here,
at any rate, progress has reached finality. There
are no more poles! None! It is so very rarely that
we can cry *Ne plus ultra!* that we must enjoy the
sensation when we can. Peary and Amundsen
hold a distinct monopoly. They are entitled to
make the most of it. The magnificent achievement
of Captain Amundsen has set us all thinking of
Arctic and Antarctic exploits. We have been trans-
ported in fancy to those lofty and jagged ranges
of mountainous ice that have been the despair of
adventurers since exploration began. We have
shivered in imagination as we have caught glimpses
of innumerable ice-floes and of stretching plains of
frozen snow. Of Captain Amundsen's success in
the south we know only the bare fact. His book,
with graphic detail and description, is a treat with
which the future tantalizes us.

But Amundsen has reminded us of Peary, and
we have picked up the Commander's book once
more. He tells a great tale. It is good to see that
the world cannot withhold its sounding applause
from the man who knows exactly where he wants

to go, and who never dreams of resting till he gets there. Peary's book is a classic of excellent leadership. Nansen told us long ago that the obstacles that intervened between civilization and the Pole, terrific as they were, were too frail for the dogged and indomitable determination of Peary. That prediction has been magnificently vindicated. Commander Peary has taught us that the really successful man is the man who knows how to keep on failing. Failure is life's high art. He who knows how to fail well will sweep everything before him. Peary kept on failing till the silver crept into his hair; and then, when well over fifty years of age, on stepping-stones of his dead self, he climbed to higher things. Through what Disraeli would have called 'the hell of failure,' he entered the heaven of his triumph.

It is ever so. The kingdom of heaven suffereth violence, and the persistent take it by storm. The conqueror is, as Wellington said, the man who never knows when he is beaten. The dust of defeat stings the face of the victor at every step of his onward march. 'The arms of the Republic,' writes Gibbon, 'often defeated in battle, were always successful in war.' 'As for Gad,' exclaimed the dying Jacob, 'a troop shall overcome him, but he shall overcome at the last.' The Cross is the last word in the grim record of the world's most ghastly failures; it is at the same time the emblem of a victory which shall shame our most radiant dreams. Those whose ears have never heard a paean, and whose brows have never felt the laurel, should ponder well this great romance of Arctic exploration. When God writes Success on any man's life He often begins to spell it with an 'f.'

Commander Peary tabulates his difficulties. Speaking generally, these coincided with Amundsen's, and they were three: (1) there was the difficulty, sometimes almost insuperable, of conveying heavy baggage over steep, ragged, slippery mountains of ice; (2) there was the difficulty presented by the piercing, penetrating, paralysing cold; (3) and there was the difficulty of the dense, depressing darkness—the long polar night. In relation to the first of these, however, we must confess that the thought that has haunted us, as we have followed our intrepid voyager, is that, really and truly, these were not the things that deterred, but the things that drove him. Their propelling power was infinitely greater than their repelling power. It is quite certain that if the Poles could have been reached in a sumptuous Pullman car, neither Peary nor Amundsen would have made the trip. It was the stupendous difficulty that lured them on.

We make an egregious blunder when we try to persuade men that the way to heaven is easy. The statement is false to fact in the first place; and, in the second, there is no responsive chord in human nature which will vibrate to that ignoble note. Hardship has a strange fascination for men. Pizarro knew what he was doing when he traced his line on the sands of Panama, and cried: "Comrades, on that side of the line are toil, hunger, nakedness, and drenching storm, desertion, and death; on this side ease and pleasure. Choose, every man! For my part, I go to the south.' Garibaldi knew what he was doing when he exclaimed: 'Soldiers, what I offer you is fatigue, danger, struggle, and death; the chill of the cold night in the free air; the intolerable heat beneath the blazing sun; no lodgings, no munitions, no provisions, but forced marches, perilous watch-posts, and the continual struggle with the bayonet against strong batteries. Those who love freedom and their country may follow me.'

Men love to be challenged and taunted and dared. Six thousand men eagerly volunteered to join Captain Scott's expedition to the South Pole. Some holding high and remunerative positions craved to be permitted to swab the decks of the *Terra Nova*. A captain in a crack cavalry regiment, with five clasps on his uniform, a hero of the South

African war, counted it an honour to perform the most menial duties at a salary of a shilling a month. Yes, Pizarro and Garibaldi, Peary and Scott knew what they were doing. They were obeying the surest instinct in the genius of leadership; for they were following Him who said: 'If any man will come after Me, let him deny himself, and take up his cross daily, and follow Me; for whosoever shall save his life shall lose it, but whosoever shall lose his life for My sake, the same shall save it.' On the road to Golgotha, the Saviour challenged the daring among men, and the heroes of all the ages have in consequence trooped to His standard.

But the colossal obstacles have often to be surmounted, Peary tells us, in the cruel cold and the dense darkness. And such cold! It is surely an allegory. Many a man feels that the task assigned him would be difficult enough in itself; but, in the chilling and disheartening atmosphere in which he has to perform it, it seems impossible. Bad enough, thought Benaiah, to fight a lion; but a lion in a pit! And a lion in a pit on a snowy day! Hard enough to persevere in well-doing when inspired by sweet whispers of gratitude, and cheered by the warm breath of sympathy. But misunderstood and unappreciated! There are millions who have discovered, with Peary, that life's heaviest loads have to be borne in the most nipping and frigid atmosphere.

And the darkness! Nobody knows what darkness is, Peary tells us, unless he has experienced an Arctic night. Week after week, with no illuming ray, the blackness seems to soak into one's very soul. But here our explorer is mistaken. There are many who have never been within thousands of miles of the Pole who nevertheless take up every morning their heavy burdens and bear them through an atmosphere more chilling than that of Arctic latitudes, and amidst darkness compared with which an Arctic night is brilliant. For there is no gloom like the petrifying gloom of mystery. The sorrows of all time reached their climax in the Man of Sorrows; and the anguish of the Christ reached its climax on the cross. And in the awful heart of that anguish there was darkness; and out from the darkness emerged the expression of eternal mystery, 'My God, My God, why hast Thou forsaken me?' The horror of the ages is concentrated in that fearful 'Why?' And with an unanswered 'Why?' upon his dumb lips, many a Christian follows his Lord in the dark.

I have said that Peary's book is a classic of distinguished leadership. This reminds me of the finest thing in the volume. The explorer makes a noble boast. In the course of his life he has led hundreds of men among Arctic foxes and Polar bears. And, save for shipping accidents that might have happened in any zone, he has brought them all safely back. There could be no more eloquent testimony to his shrewd foresight, his unfailing diligence, and his almost fond unselfishness, than that. Of nothing is he more proud. But Peary's leadership is modelled on a greater. What though at times the burdens of life seem crushing? What though the atmosphere seem paralysing? What though the darkness seem appalling? *He* leads on. He has felt the darkness and the cold. The responsibility is, after all, in the last resort, upon the leader. And, with unerring wisdom and beautiful accuracy of judgment, He picks out the perilous path and apportions the difficult tasks to the well-known potentialities of His followers. 'Of those whom Thou hast given Me,' He says, 'I have lost none.' Commander Peary's great book has taught us that the wise leader sets an infinite value on the welfare of his most lowly follower; and that every task is allotted in the light of that lofty estimate.

IX

HAT-PINS AND BUTTON-HOOKS

I HAVE been reading a pretty tale of a wee lassie, who, on bounding in from school, exclaimed that she had learned to punctuate. 'Indeed!' exclaimed her mother, 'and how do you do it, Elsie?' 'Well, mamma,' cried the excited little grammarian, 'it's just as easy as easy can be! If you say that a thing *is* so, you just put a *hat-pin* after it; but if you are only asking whether it is so or not, you put a *button-hook*!'

On thinking it over, we have reached the deliberate conclusion that there is a world of sound philosophy about the little lassie's explanation. All life resolves itself, sooner or later, into a matter of hat-pins and button-hooks. If we were to hold a kind of mental spring-cleaning, turning out all the drawers of memory and cupboards of thought; if we were to sort out all our notions and ideas, our doctrines and our theories; if we were to overhaul our entire intellectual and moral equipment, we should discover with surprise that the great bulk of

it all could be sharply divided under these two heads
—our affirmations and our interrogations; the
things of which we are positive, and the things of
which we are doubtful; the matters on which we are
dogmatic and the matters on which we are dubious.
The soul has a stock-in-trade of its own; and on its
shelves are to be found the goods that it has bought
outright and the goods of which it has accepted
delivery on probation. We carry these two classes
of stores—our certainties and our suspicions—
these and no others. Our cupboards are crammed,
that is to say, with hat-pins and with button-hooks.

It is in these two classes of goods that the churches
do their main business. The Church makes great
affirmations, and she propounds great interroga-
tions. She declares confidently: *We know* whom we
have believed! *We know* that all things work to-
gether for good! *We know* that, if our earthly
house were destroyed, we have a house not made
with hands, eternal in the heavens! She asks great
questions too: What shall it profit a man? How
shall we escape if we neglect? What shall the end
be of those that obey not the gospel? Surely the
pulpit is of all places the natural home of stupend-
ous affirmation and searching interrogation.

Oliver Wendell Holmes rushes to the memory at
once. ' "I will agree," said Number Seven, "to write

the history of two worlds, this and the next, in such a compact way that you can commit them both to memory in less time than you can learn the answer to the first question in the catechism." He took a blank card from his pocket-book, and wrote:

$$\frac{\mathbf{!}}{\mathbf{?}}$$

' "Two worlds! Endless doubt and unrest here below; wondering, admiring, adoring certainty above. Am I not right?" ' It was conceded that he *was* right. It comes to this. The story of two worlds can be set forth by a single hat-pin and a single button-hook.

Hat-pins and button-hooks are both very good in their way, and for their proper purposes. We have heard of hat-pins being used with vicious intent at football matches and in street riots, just as we have heard men speak with certainty where they would have been wiser to have spoken with caution. They were cock-sure; but time has shown that they were wrong. It was an abuse of the hat-pin, that was all. 'Have your beliefs,' says an old writer, 'and have your doubts. Believe your beliefs, and doubt your doubts. Never doubt your beliefs, and never believe

your doubts.' It is a quaint way of saying that
the hat-pin and the button-hook must be kept, each
in its proper place, and must be used, each for its
proper purpose.

In a magnificent lecture delivered to students
not long before his death, Dr. John Watson urged
the importance of this very thing. There are certain
matters, he contended, on which the preacher can
be absolutely positive—the facts of Revelation, of
the Deity of the Son of God, of Sin, of Redemp-
tion, and of the power of the Holy Ghost. Round
these splendid facts, he demonstrated, there revolved
a thousand theories. Between these things he en-
treated the students to distinguish clearly. *'The
facts,'* he said, 'should be declared in faith with
much assurance; *the theories* should be advanced as
contributing light with diffidence.'

The button-hook, like the hat-pin, is a most useful
article in its own way. It is a good thing to ask
questions. It was the occupation of the child Jesus
in the midst of the doctors. Towards the close of
his life Dr. Thomas Guthrie wrote a beautiful letter
to his daughter congratulating her on her first ap-
proach to the table of the Lord. The letter simply
overflows with intense affection and fatherly coun-
sel. And it contains this pertinent passage: 'I saw
an adage yesterday, in a medical magazine, which is

well worth your remembering and acting on.   It is
this wise saying of the great Lord Bacon's: WHO
ASKS MUCH, LEARNS MUCH.   I remember the day
when I did not like, by asking, to confess my igno-
rance.   I have long given up that, and now seize on
every opportunity of adding to my stock of knowl-
edge.   Now don't forget Lord Bacon's wise saying!'
There are only two men in the whole wide world
who can ask questions effectively.   There is the
man who does not know, and wants to learn; and
there is the man who does know, and wants to
teach.   Of the former, Alexander the Great is the
classical illustration; among the latter, Socrates
stands supreme.   We all remember the great passage
in Plutarch, in which the rise of Alexander is largely
attributed to his endless facility for asking sagacious
questions.   When Frank Buckland, the delightful
naturalist, was in his fourth year, his mother wrote
of him: 'He is always asking questions.   If there
is anything he cannot understand, he won't go on
till it has been explained to him.   There is no end
to his questions.'   And Dr. Culross, in his exquisite
monogram of Carey, tells us how the 'sensible lad
in the leather apron' attracted the notice of Dr. Scott,
the commentator, by his 'modest asking of appro-
priate questions.'

The place of the button-hook is permanent.   So

long as life throbs with mystery the place of the interrogation is assured. The baby asks questions as soon as he can prattle.

> Why, muvver, why
> Was those poor blackbirds all baked in a pie?
> And why did the cow jump right over the moon?
> And why did the dish run away with the spoon?
> And why must we wait for our wings till we die?
> Why, muvver, why?

And death comes at last, and finds us still asking the old questions:

> Why?
> This is the cry
> That echoes through the wilderness of earth,
> Through song and sorrow, day of death and birth:
> Why?

> Why?
> It is the high
> Wail of the child with all his life to face;
> Man's last dumb question as he reaches space:
> Why?

The comfort about it all is that the really big things of life are represented by hat-pins, and only the things that can afford to wait by button-hooks. Dr. Dale used to illustrate this by a reference to the pillars beside his pulpit. 'It appears to you,' he would say to the congregation at Carr's Lane, 'that these pillars support this arch above my head. They do nothing of the kind. If you could stand where I stand, you would see that they have been cut through to make room for this rostrum, and they actually hang upon the arch which they seem to support.' In like fashion, our faith seems at times to depend upon the theories and evidences concerning which we ask our questions. In point of fact, it does nothing of the kind. If all our theories and evidences were cut through like the pillars, our faith would still stand securely like the arch. Our certainties infinitely outnumber and outweigh our speculations. *We know.* The soul plants her feet on a sure refuge of her own. Professor Forsyth rightly argues that to the individual consciousness there can be no stronger witness than its own experience of the love of God, of the merits of the Saviour's Cross, and of the efficacy of His risen power. These the soul takes into stock, not on approbation, but for ever and for all. She buys these truths and sells them not. The Christian gospel holds for the believer stupendous and satisfying certainties; and, amidst these affirmations, secure from all interrogations, the heart loves to build its nest.

X

THE BROW OF THE HILL

THE brow of the hill has a divinity of its own. There is something distinctly spiritual, as well as something distinctly sublime, about a summit. That is why the heathen loved to build their altars there. How often, in the historical books of the Old Testament, we are told that the idolatrous people erected their shrines and raised their images on the high hills about Jerusalem! How the Aztecs delighted in rearing their strange temples, shaped like pyramids, on the loftiest peaks of Mexico, with the altar on the topmost pinnacle of the temple! And the same sure instinct has led men to lay their bones to rest on the brow of the hill. They wearily sought its silent and solemn sanctity at the last! We have all visited, at least in fancy, the resting-place of Robert Louis Stevenson. 'Nothing more picturesque can be imagined,' his cousin tells us, 'than the narrow ledge that forms the summit of Vaea, a place no wider than a room, and flat as a table. On either side the land descends precipitously; in front lies the vast ocean with the surf-swept reefs; to the right and left green mountains rise, densely covered with the primaeval forest.' No firearms must be discharged about those slopes. The chiefs insist that the birds must be undisturbed, that they 'may raise about his grave the songs he loved so well.' I saw the other day a striking picture of Cecil Rhodes's lonely grave on the crest of the mighty Matoppos in Africa. Two lions from the valley beneath are standing on the great flat tomb, and seem in harmony with the wild, romantic place.

But I no longer hold the attention of my readers. Their thoughts have left Robert Louis Stevenson and Cecil Rhodes far behind, and have visited the strange, lone resting-place of Moses among the mountains of Moab.

> That was the grandest funeral
> That ever passed on earth;
> But no man heard the trampling,
> Or saw the train go forth.
> Perchance the bald old eagle
> On grey Beth-peor's height,
> Out of his rocky eyrie
> Looked on the wondrous sight.

And Browning has expressed the same fondness for a mountain burial in his 'Grammarian's Funeral.'

Here's the top peak; the multitude below
    Live, for they can, there:
This man decided not to live but know—
    Bury this man there?
Here—here's his place, where meteors shoot, clouds form,
    Lightnings are loosened,
Stars come and go! Let joy break with the storm!
    Peace let the dew send!
Lofty designs must close in like effects:
    Loftily lying,
Leave him—still loftier than the world suspects,
    Living and dying.

Now I have simply pointed to these altars and monuments that deck the hill-tops of the world in order to prove that there exists, in the very blood of the race, an instinctive reverence for the brow of the hill. We feel that summits are sacred. Why? That is the question. Let us investigate.

Now, in attempting a solution of this alluring mystery, I must call to my aid two gentlemen of rare insight and of profound scholarship— Professor George Adam Smith and Mr. A. C. Benson. In treating of the 121st Psalm the learned Principal says: 'To the psalmist the mountains spread a threshold for a divine arrival. Up there God Himself may be felt to be afoot. Whether we climb them, or gaze at them, the mountains produce in us that mingling of moral and physical emotion in which the temper of true worship

consists.' So much for the Principal. Now for the
schoolmaster. 'It is good,' writes Mr. Benson, in
one of his delightful essays, 'it is good for the *body*
to climb the steep slopes and breathe the pure air;
it is good for the *mind* to see the map of the coun-
try fairly unrolled before the eye; and it is good
for the *soul,* too, to see the world lie extended at
one's feet. How difficult it is to analyze the vague
and poignant emotions which then and thus arise!'
'A hill-top,' remarks another writer, 'is a moral as
well as a physical elevation.'

Now it is as clear as clear can be that the hunger
of our hearts for the hills is only a part of the
hunger of our hearts for the infinite. The instinct
of the far horizon is indelibly engraven in our very
nature. Go where you will, visit what city you like,
and you will straightway be taken to some noble and
commanding eminence *to see the view.* Surely this
phenomenon requires some explanation. Even the
most intelligent of the lower animals betray no love
for the landscape. They know nothing of the pas-
sion of the far horizon. I have often ascended
Mount Wellington, at Hobart, and gazed entranced
upon the magnificent panorama of land and sea
that unrolls itself, in altogether indescribable
grandeur, at one's feet. The prospect is almost over-
powering. But I have noticed repeatedly that,

whilst every member of the party turns in ecstasy to admire so glorious a landscape, the horses and dogs —man's most intelligent and sagacious companions —have deliberately turned their backs upon the magnificent landscape, to forage for food on the bushy slopes near by. The different behaviour of the men and the animals is much more than a matter of *degree.* It is a contrast in *kind.* It is a direct line of cleavage. It is arresting and inviting.

In one of his most captivating and suggestive passages, Mark Rutherford, in his *Revolution in Tanner's Lane,* tells how the boys of the tiny hamlet of Cowfold would, on a holiday, trudge the three dusty miles down the lane from the village to the main coach road, and back again, just for the rapture of reading the wondrous words 'TO LONDON,' 'TO YORK,' on the finger-post at the end of the lane. The romance of the mysterious fingers pointing mutely down the winding road along which the coaches rattled on their way to the great capitals, was 'an opening into infinity,' to use Mark Rutherford's words, to the boys of Cowfold. It was the next best thing to a mountain peak. It is so with every boy. The instinct of the far horizon burns within him. He reads Jules Verne and R. M. Ballantyne, Captain Marryat and Captain Mayne Reid, G. A. Henty and Gordon Stables. These are his classics. He glories in boundless plains and impenetrable jungles; in pathless prairies and endless snows; in trackless deserts and illimitable oceans. He revels in a limitless landscape. His fertile fancy converts every hencoop and dog-kennel into a wigwam or a kraal, every paddock into a prairie, every terrier into a tiger, and the boys of every neighbouring school into a fierce and hostile tribe. He is always on an imaginary hill-top, looking out upon the four corners of the earth. He loathes the intimate and loves the infinite. There is evidently some subtle and mysterious ingredient in his composition that is totally absent in the make-up of your noblest horses and your finest dogs. The passion of the wide horizon, the instinct of the infinite, the spirit of the summit, tingles in his very blood.

Yet, after all, it must be sorrowfully confessed that the hill-tops never really satisfy. The horizon is always small, the landscape limited. We look out to sea, and we wonder what ships are sailing out there beyond the skyline; we gaze across the land, and we wonder what lies beyond the distant ranges.

> The peak is high, and flushed
>   At its highest with sunrise fire;
> The peak is high and the stars are high,
>   But the thought of man is higher.

Yet be quite sure that the hunger that the highest peak leaves unsatisfied is no mockery. It is to appease it that the churches live. For there is another hill-top. 'Then said the Shepherds one to another, "Let us here show to the pilgrims the gates of the Celestial City." The pilgrims then lovingly accepted the motion. So they had them to the top of a high hill, called Clear, and gave them their glass to look. And they saw some of the glory of the place. Then they went away and sang this song:

"Thus by the Shepherds secrets are revealed,
Which from all other men are kept concealed:
Come to the Shepherds then, if you would see
Things deep, things hid, and that mysterious be." '

Let all the Shepherds of all the flocks take note. The hunger for the hilltop is a very real and a very beautiful thing. It is not satisfied by rearing altars there. It is not appeased by planning, like Stevenson and Rhodes, to lie in stately silence there. There is no mountain-peak among earth's loftiest ranges high enough to gratify the cravings of a single soul. The view is so restricted. Men are hungry for the wealthier vision that is to be seen from the summit of the hill called Clear; and it is for the Shepherds to take these wistful pilgrims there.

CPSIA information can be obtained
at www.ICGtesting.com
Printed in the USA
BVOW10s0937251117
500833BV00030B/493/P